LIFE in the MEZZOGIORNO:
'MONGST GAZING GARGOYLES

By Anne Condra

Messapici Publishing

The Interior view of the *Del'Aquila Villa*
is by Giorgio Aguglia, Leece, Italy
and I want to thank him for the privilege
of using his beautiful sketch in this work.

All other sketches and book jacket design
are mine and are under copyright.

Some of the Italian language used in this text,
particularily the dialect, is expressed in the way I
heard it, not necessarily in proper Italian or for
that matter proper Leccese!

Published in the United States of America
by Messapici Publishing, Springfield, Illinois.
Library of Congress Catalog Number 97-92577
Condra, Ann
Life in the Mezzogiorno : 'Mongst Gazing Gargoyles
ISBN C-9660568-0-9
First Edition 1997
Printed by Rudin Printing Company, Inc., Springfield, Illinois.
Messapici Publishing

Bibliography

Alvino, Ernesto, *Un Giorno A Lecce,*
Salentina - Galatina (LE) Italia1983.

Fagiolo, Marcello & Cazzato, Vincenzo,
Ediitori Laterza & Figli, *Le città nellastoria
d'Italia LECCE,* Spa Roma-Bari, Italia1988.

Palumbo, Pietro, STORIA DI LECCE,
Biblioteca di cultura Pugliese,
fondata e diretta da Michele Paone, 1981.
Edizioni DE VERGORI, LECCE città barocca,
Lecci, Italy

DEDICATED TO

ANTONIO ALBERONE
1931-1996
and *i vicini.* (the neighbors)
Whose spirits inspired this *lovoro fatto con amore.* (My labor of love.)

MY SPECIAL THANKS TO

MARTA BOLOGNINI AGUGLIA
Who taught, nurtured and befriended me.

LIFE in the MEZZOGIORNO:
'MONGST GAZING GARGOYLES

By Anne Condra

Messapici *Publishing*

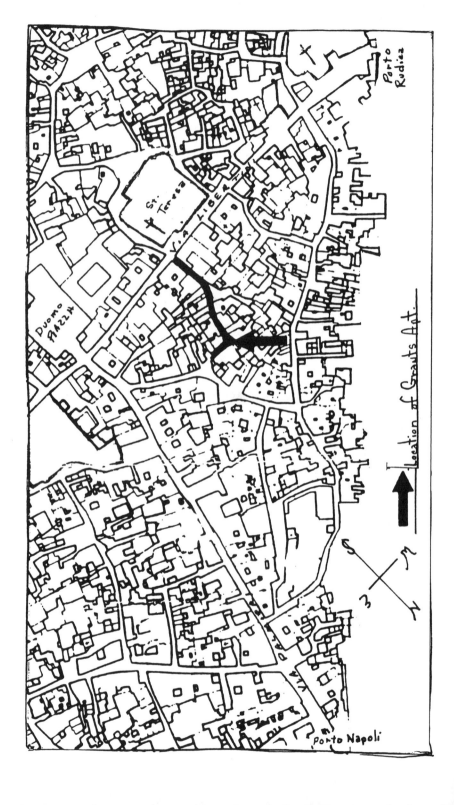

St. Teresa

VIA LIBEA

Duomo
PIAZZA

Porto
Rudiza

Location of Grants Apt.

Porto Napoli

VIA

Preface

It must have been pre-ordained for us to have the experience of living in Lecce, located in the heel of Italy, with a particular group of people and at a specific time. The experiences of that adventure have delighted, inspired, and motivated me to record them so I can ward off dreaded forgetfulness and share with others, hopefully infecting them with this virus of enthusiasm for the Mezzogiorno that I have lived with and can't seem to shake off or find a cure for since returning to the Midwest, in America. Perhaps a remedy will never be found, and I will be allowed the luxury of indulging in this lovely disorder every time I'm reminded of a little corner of the world that was ours for three years.

The setting is a picturesque scene of three-hundred-year-old architecture quaint enough to make me drool when I was shown the apartment. Unbeknownst to my husband and myself, our lives were no longer to be our own, as we were tethered to the inhabitants of these stone corridors the moment we signed the lease. There nothing happens that is so miniscule as to not be noticed and reported. The paparazzi, international wire services, database and the internet can offer nothing compared to the expertise of this little neighborly network of broadcasters in their quest for knowledge. Whether it was pre-ordained is not important, but I'm grateful it wasn't left out of my life experience.

chiesa di Sant'Irene

Part I
Old World Hazing

1

It is May 1987, another large company in the American Midwest is meeting its demise. It is in a comatose state just waiting for the final yank of the plug before it can be put to rest and the remnant of employees can get on with their lives elsewhere. An engineering department which employed close to three hundred people has dwindled to thirty. Some have retired, others are asked to take an early retirement; occasionally incentives are offered and at other times not; some are just let go and some are asked to move to the other side of the world where the parent company has their principle operations.

Our relocation is initiated by the company's management in Italy. They cannot entice northern Italian engineers to relocate to the plant in the South. There is a social stigma about living south of an imaginary line drawn somewhere between Rome and Naples. The southern side covers the remaining part of the peninsula and Sicily; it is known as the Mezzogiorno (noon), denoting a time of day when all commerce shuts down for a large meal and *riposo* (afternoon nap). The Mezzogiorno is a label that suggests laziness. The Northerners feel that too much of their tax money goes to support the agrarian South. It is also referred to as "Little Africa," and the natives *Africani*. So, the choice given to a few Americans is move to southern Italy or find other employment. It is a typical Italian offer, one that is hard to refuse.

Of the dozen men who are asked to relocate, only a few have accumulated thirty years with the company. Most of the others could achieve that goal however, by signing the three-year contract and moving to the Mezzogiorno. The significance of acquiring thirty years is the endowment of a small pension and more importantly, medical benefits. These are high priorities to those of us facing a fiftieth birthday and unemployment!

Three couples and one man accept the challenge of the three-year contract and begin a new adventure in Italy's heel on the Adriatic seacoast in mid-January 1988. A fourth couple, Burt and Anita Rossiter, is assigned to Torino. We are uprooted and cast into the midst of sights, sounds, scents and struggles unfamiliar to our midwestern upbringing.

Finding ourselves in Lecce, Italy, is as mind-boggling to the seven of us midwesterners and our Irish setter, as was Oz to the little girl from Kansas and her devoted canine companion. Bridget's unwavering companionship is a source of comfort to us that cannot be equaled. No longer are we basking in the luxury of self-sufficiency; language skills have to be acquired without delay.

Knowledge of the language is first priority and becomes a consuming preoccupation. A tutor is hired by the company six months before the move. Learning vocabulary and forming new sounds correctly is time consuming, frustrating, and thoroughly exhausting. The inability to communicate leads to emotional effects as well as culture shock. We manage, however, to recover from timidity, painful nervousness, and fear of humiliation by sharing experiences among ourselves. This results in a very special camaraderie. Humor is oftentimes a healer and restorer. Our enthusiasm for living in the mild climate of romantic, ancient Italy is short-lived, and annoyances set in as soon as discovery is made of the drastic differences between American and southern Italian culture.

2

We arrive at the Aeroporto di Brindisi on January 13, 1988. The temperature is a mild fifty-two degrees on this Wednesday evening as the four of us step onto Italian soil, quite a drastic change from the frigid air in Chicago at O'Hare Airport the day before. Sharing the tiresome twenty-six hour journey with me, Gaines, and our dog are Norma and Tom Browning. A sense of euphoria replaces our weariness felt on the flight down from Rome.

"Look, Adrianne, the geraniums are in full bloom!" Norma points down to the long, narrow strip of soil which is a flower garden between the sidewalk and the terminal building. "If we were home, we wouldn't see them for months!"

Inside the small airport a welcoming committee of two drivers and a secretary-hostess, sent by the company, are waiting to drive us to Lecce, which is twenty-five miles south.

"*Buona sera e benvenuti*" (good evening and welcome), I am Signora Bellafiore and I would like to introduce you all to our company drivers for this evening, Signore Verdi and Signore Gatti." We shake hands and say, "*Piacere*" (pleased to meet you), voicing our own identities.

Two huge German shepherds bounce toward us, leading armed guards. Signora Bellafiore notices our concerned looks and says, "Don't be alarmed, they are here to sniff out drugs."

We congregate by the conveyor belt anxiously awaiting the arrival of Bridget and our luggage. The clicking sound activates the belt and Gaines squeezes my hand as we wait for the first glimpse of our Irish setter. The plastic caddy comes into view and the dog whines in response to her master's voice, which escalates to ear-piercing shrillness until she is freed. She bathes

3

Gaines' hands with her soft, warm tongue, wagging her backside vigorously.

"She seems all right," Gaines says, as he examines her and the inside of the caddy.

"She looks good," Tom adds, giving her auburn coat a few admiring strokes.

Bridget pushes her nose into my thighs. "I'm so happy to see you I was afraid they would send you to Bangkok or Calcutta."

On the top of the caddy is the information that Gaines had taped to it before leaving home. We look on with amusement as we read:

Mi chiama Bridget	My name is Bridget
Io ho 2-1/2 anni, femmina	I am 2-1/2 years, female
Sto viaggiando verso Roma	I am flying to Rome, Italy
Lecce, Italy è la mia	Lecce, Italy is my
destinazione	destination
Il 13 Gennaio 1988	13 January 1988
I miei Padroni sono I Signori	My owners are Mr. & Mrs
Gaines Grant	Gaines Grant
Via dei Sepolcri	Via dei Sepolcri
Messapici - 24	Messapici - 24
Lecce, Italia	Lecce, Italy
73100	73100
Numeri dei voli	Flight Numbers
BM 0387 & AZ6668	BM 0387 & AZ6668

Norma pats the dog's soft head and neck, admiring her beautiful brown eyes. "You're all right, Bridgie. I wish I had brought our dachshund, Holly, but she will be happy with our daughter and her husband." Norma gives Bridget a hug.

Tom lifts their last bag from the belt, handing it to Signore Verdi, saying, "Well, that's it for us!"

4

"I see our last two coming now. Well, maybe this is a good omen. We're here, unscathed including canine and luggage," observes Gaines.

Tom grins at me and Norma. "There's no turning back now, girls!"

"Scary, isn't it, Norma? Our houses are sold, furniture in storage. It's almost like starting over."

"Don't remind me!" Norma is worried. "We'll get in touch *domani*," Tom says, changing the subject, and with a wave he and Norma follow their driver out of the terminal.

"*Arrivederci!*" we respond.

The Brownings go to the Hotel Tiziano, which will be home until they can find an apartment. The company is giving them a month at the hotel.

Signora Bellafiore sits in the front seat with the driver. Bridgie snuggles up on the second seat between me and Gaines, basking in our affectionate pats and occasional hugs as we ride into Porta Napoli, one of several sixteenth-century gates of the historic district of Lecce.

Our attention is enticed outside of the van to the variance of lifestyles exhibited in the street. Vendors from Morocco and Cameroon are wrapped from head to toe in colorful fabric, inquiring of passersby, "*vu compri?*" (Do you want to buy?) trinkets and cassettes.

A Franciscan Monk dressed in the traditional brown-hooded habit and sandals has been knocked over on his bicycle by a zealous driver and both have become the center of attention, shouting their own defenses at one another. Bystanders take sides and liven up the evening's activity for everyone near.

Prostitutes soliciting in the vicinity of the gate under the giant umbrella pines are flashing at the motorists. "Welcome to Lecce," Gaines remarks as we snicker at the spectacle.

The cosmopolitan environment stimulates our enthusiasm for our new home. We admire the Old World charm of the street scene in silence as the driver impatiently dodges pedestrians, motor scooters, dogs and baby carriages. His annoyance is exhibited by shouts of damnation and gestures that have as much meaning as the spoken word. Maneuvering up the crowded, one-way incline, he abruptly makes a sharp right turn, tossing us to the opposite side of the van. Not troubling himself to reduce speed for a parked car ahead, he shoots through the restricted space like a demon, Gaines turns around exhaling in relief. "I wonder by how many millimeters the company's van was spared?" he whispers.

Suddenly, the driver takes a left at a Y-shaped intersection in a more open area and we are thrown to the right, nearly shoving us to the floor. Just having recovered our upright positions, he swerves again to the right, this time to miss the poor soul who is sanding a table in the street in front of a refinishing shop. "Oh, my!" I gasp, as we enter a smaller passageway barely wide enough for the van. Signora Bellafiore cautions, *"Piano, piano"* (slowly, slowly). It seems to incite this devil-may-care driver, and for reasons known only to the Almighty he accelerates for about forty-five meters. His two available choices are to collide with the house ahead or try for a ninety-degree left turn. I bury my face in Bridget's neck, while Gaines holds my shoulder with one hand and grips the edge of his seat with the other.

Relieved and thanking God that he has finessed the turn, he slams the brakes jolting us forward. Shaken and too dazed to observe the gentle shift in reverse, the driver brings the vehicle to a delicate stop in front of the iron gate. He turns around flashing a smile and says, *"Va bene."* (It goes well.) I press my hand on the back of my neck and ask. "How does one say whiplash and chiropractor in Italian?"

Signora Bellafiore gives the driver a good dressing-down in words, phrases and gestures executed with a velocity that escapes our understanding, but her intention is well perceived by us. He shakes his head as if he can't possibly understand why she is upset. She turns around and says to us, " He has been to a professional driving school and takes pleasure in showing us his skills. There is an expression here: "If you don't like the way I drive, get off the sidewalk!"

Stumbling out of the van, Gaines and I use each other as supports to gain equilibrium when we notice the white, twelve foot-facade of Via dei Sepolcri Messapici, number twenty-four. This seventeenth-century apartment will be our little corner of the world for the next three years. The Signora unlocks the security gate taking care to draw attention to the small step down into the *porte-co-chère*, a sheltered carriage entrance leading into an open courtyard. Usually a room or walkway above provides the covering. She leads us into the walled, three-storied enclosure that unfolds gradually and gains width at the outside stairs.

The entrance to the ground floor flat is about two-and-a-half meters from the bottom of the slightly curved staircase. A dark green painted metal handrail ascends with eighteen very steep stone steps leading to the apartment, which is on the second and third floors.

Signora Bellafiore unlocks the dark green paneled, oval-topped door and turns the heavy brass knob. She is first inside and we follow her down the long hallway and into the spacious dining room. She looks all around, "Ahhh, cheee bellllaaa!" (How beautiful!) It is said with such exaggeration it is difficult not to smile. "Signore Gatti is bringing the luggage and caddy. That is a job he is suited for," she says, reflecting on his driving performance.

A welcoming bouquet of mixed flowers has been placed in the center of a round, inlayed-marble dining room tabletop, which rests on elegant black cast-iron legs. The refrigerator is stocked, and the heat turned on to take the chill out of the stone house.

"Isn't it beautiful? Oh, Gaines, I love it! It has always been a fantasy of mine to live in a house like this. I'm afraid I'll wake up and this will be just a lovely dream."

"Yes, it is beautiful. I want you to be content over here. You're doing what a lot of American women wouldn't. You'll be alone a lot. Of course, you'll have Bridgie." He stoops to stroke the dog.

I admire the aqua painted baseboards dividing the light marble flooring from the expanse of white walls. "How high do you think the ceilings are?" Gaines cocks his head and looks around. "Close to thirteen feet."

The handsome dark antique chests and colorful oriental rugs bring warmth to the rooms and complement the floral design of the slipcovered love seats.

The corner fireplace in the living room is smooth stone. Signora Bellafiore admires it and points to a twenty-one-inch antique puppet hanging from the mantle. "This is Orlando Furioso. He is from Sicilian folklore and it is believed that he brings good luck to the house where he guards the hearth." He has a china face and a little disarranged wig giving him a comical look. He is dressed in armor, helmet with a red plume, red cape trimmed with gold fringe, and a sword dangles at his side.

"How interesting. Our landlady has furnished this house well. I feel fortunate to have found it."

Signore Gatti carries the caddy inside. Gaines says, "Just put it outside the kitchen on the patio and thanks for your help."

Bridget walks ahead of us to the door, swishing her tail high in the air, which resembles a large burnt sienna plume. The Signora and the driver pet her wavy red coat, and we all say goodnight.

Gaines and I wander through the strangely laid out house, finding light switches, the thermostat and circuit breaker, familiarizing ourselves with the uncertain and changing layout. There had never been a plan, it just evolved over time.

"If anyone had to write a legal description of this place, I honestly don't know how they'd do it!" Gaines says, shaking his head. " The guest bedroom is off by itself over the porte-co-chère, and the only bathroom on this floor is at the other end of the house. Before we have overnight guests, Adrianne, we'll have to buy some night lights. If our guests get up at night, they'll have to go down this long hallway past the kitchen alcove

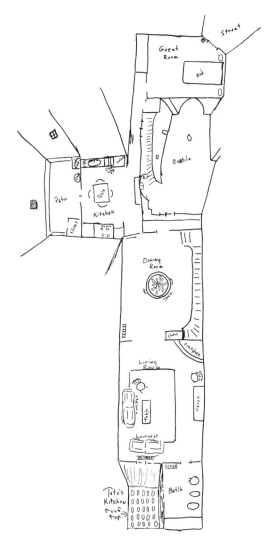

Piano Primo, first floor plan.

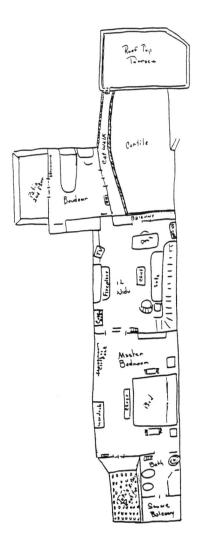

Piano Secondo, second floor plan.

and step down into the dining room, walk through both the dining and living rooms to get to the bath. Looking at it, I'd say about nineteen meters. Whew!" He shakes his head. "What a place!"

"I know, but think of living in a house with marble floors, high ceilings, French doors to balconies, a rooftop terrace, stone fireplaces and furnished with antiques!"

"Adrianne, you are an incurable romantic. I'd trade a little bit of this elegance for a garage and a yard."

Street Sweeper.

3

I wake up and look at Gaines and Bridget curled up together, the dog contentedly snoring with her little red head resting on Gaines' arm. Knowing that Bridget will soon wake to the call of nature and no longer have a convenient, fenced backyard, I hurry to dress so I can escort Bridget to our new surroundings. Standing on the widest part of the narrowest stone street I have ever seen, I notice evidence of where other dogs have found relief. The filth is disgusting. Not only manure, but partially eaten spaghetti is piled on a sack beside the house across the street.

A few meters from us a flock of pigeons pick up stale bread pieces. Their luxuriant variegated coats exhibit hues of violet, blue, slate and beige. My free hand is deep inside a plastic bag ready to collect Bridget's excrement, but before my task is accomplished, we hear a menacing, alien racket. The threat is a three-wheeled scooter with large, dark grey, plastic bins fastened to the frame allowing just enough room for the driver who is positioned behind the refuse-filled receptacles. He is a city employee hired to make early rounds and sweep the streets. His primitive broom looks homemade from vines or small twigs resembling a Halloween witch's contrivance used to make nocturnal flights across a full, orange colored harvest moon. The street sweeper uses a long-handled dustpan to catch the debris, depositing it in one of the bins. Mounting the conveyance, he works in cycles of repetition. There is a radical difference between the sight before me and the huge machines used in the States -- unbelievably primitive.

The quaint, Old World setting is enhanced by bougainvillea issuing delicately shaped petals of vivid crimson

13

and magenta. These vines are competing for space on the walls and iron railings with hardy wisteria laden with clusters of lavender blossoms.

Drawn back to reality, I abandon the desire to soak up more of the setting for fear my shoulder will suffer dislocation. I struggle to keep my salivating pet from lunging to the leftover spaghetti. "Let's go back in, Bridgie."

Slightly out of breath and thirty-six steps later, I reach the master bedroom on the third floor and find Gaines almost dressed for work. He folds down the collar of the blue, oxford cloth shirt. Fastening the buttons he says, "The driver will be here soon to take me out to the office."

"Is it the same one we had last night?"

"Sì."

"You can't seriously think about riding with that maniac again." Reflecting on his performance last night, I shudder as I sit on the unmade bed.

"We'll just have to get used to it. They all drive like that. Remember what Signora Bellafiore said last night? 'If you don't like the way I drive, get off the sidewalk!' "

"I'm too young to be a widow! What in the world would I do if something happened to you?"

"You're saying that it would be okay at home, but not here?"

"Don't twist my meaning. At least at home I'd know what to do. Seriously, we've never talked about <u>that</u> before coming over here. I wouldn't even know who to call!"

"Oh, just bury me in Iowa."

"Mamma mia! It would be simpler to cremate you here and sprinkle your ashes in Iowa."

"If you cremate me, I'll come back and haunt you."

"Well, if you bury me in Iowa, I'll come back and haunt you!"

We walk to the front door, kiss goodbye and embrace as Bridget tries to pry us apart with her nose.

14

"Now, be careful of the cars, if you decide to go out today."

"I will, don't worry."

"I love you, and I'll try to be home early. Bridgie, be a good dog and take care of Mom." He gives the dog a pat.

"I love you, too. Take care. I'll pray for you."

"Oh! I need it! Arrivederci!"

"*Ci vediamo, Caro.*" (We will see each other, dear.)

I go into the guest room, open the French doors and look down onto the street. Gaines gets into the company car. Lord, protect him, I pray, as he zooms out of sight.

Pondering my inevitable task at hand, knowing I have to start some time, I prepare to leave the house. "I just hope I can find this place again in my lifetime, Bridget. It might be wise to blaze a trail."

There was no plan regarding the way the streets had been laid out. I heard an Italian explain that when the old cities were built, they were purposely developed to be confusing so as to thwart pirates and marauders who raided on a regular basis. It was almost impossible for them to find their way out once they had ventured into the maze of stone.

Approaching the end of the street and no longer having a view of the front gate, I decide to turn around, but then I notice a shop on the corner. The entrance is on the intersecting street and after I turn the corner, facing me over the door is the word *SALUMERIA* in large, red block lettering. Oh, a delicatessen. The permeating aromas of cheese, mortadella and marinated vegetables greet me as I enter. The door closes behind me, causing a bell to sound. Noticing a new customer enter his one room domain, the proprietor scurries around the meat case which faces the door at the end of the cluttered, disorganized, product-filled room.

He is short, stocky and in his early fifties. He wipes his greasy hands on a cloth and slings it over the shoulder of his long, white butcher's coat. He hastens toward me in a businesslike manner, infringing on my comfort zone. He thrusts his face in mine motioning with a raised hand, fingers and thumb pressed together, demanding *"Dimmi Signora."* (Tell me, Mrs.) The intrusiveness causes me to tilt backward, while I try to translate his speedy opening statement. With a push of his upper body, he lunges and shoots at me again.

"Oh! Oh! Okay, now! I know what you are asking, well a..." Forming my first word, "Vorrei" (I would like), I attempt to create a little more space between us and step backward only to have him follow my lead. His body heat and garlic breath momentarily sap my concentration.   I prefer more space and casually ease to the side, but my subtlety escapes Mario as he determinedly pursues my side step and begins shouting guesses at me. *"Pomodori?"* (Tomatoes.) Accompanying my back step he bellows, *"Pane?"* (Bread.) We dance around the limited floor space, *"Latte?"* (Milk.) His wife, Beatrice, seated behind the cash register chimes in yelling *"Formaggio?"* (Cheese.) *"Burro?"* (Butter.)

The frolic comes to an abrupt end when I stumble over a large can of olive oil behind me on the floor, but Mario, ever so close, prevents the fall by catching my elbow. *"Grazie Signore."* (Thanks Mr.) I remove my arm from Mario's grip and regain my composure, verbalizing my first Italian phrase to a native. *"Vorrei un etto di parmigiano e grattugiato, per favore."* (I would like a fourth pound of parmigiano, grated, please.) Completing the lengthy spiel, I exhale in relief.

My audience stands frozen before me, eyes fixed on my novice performance. His head is held forward, mouth ajar, he gives his head such an uncontrollable shaking that anyone outside the shop could easily hear the flapping sound of his sizably endowed jowls. Mario's rude animation of not understanding a word I have uttered is well perceived. Brushing his antics aside, I walk to the meat case and point to the large wheel of parmigiano saying, *"Un etto."*

"Ahhhhhhh! Sì, sì, sì, sì, sì!" He excitedly runs around the case. *"Lei preferisce grattugiato o un pezzo?"* (Do you prefer grated or a piece?) Again his question wings past my comprehension like speeding bullets.

My desire to imitate his impolite, shaking wet-dog charade is briefly contemplated, but permission is denied and I diplomatically say, *"Piano, piano, Signore. Io non capisco bene."* (Speak slowly. I don't understand well.)

Ignoring my request, he continues with the same velocity, but speaks a few octaves higher. How absurd, and I try to control pent-up laughter. He thinks amplification aids comprehension. 'Oh, if only it did!' Using a little guess work, I pantomime by moving my right fist back and forth over my flat left palm, responding to what I assume he has asked.

"Ahhhhhhhh! Sì, sì, sì, sì, sì,!" Flamboyantly, he takes the wooden-handled, steel, pie-shaped cheese breaker. Securing my full attention, he inserts the special utensil into the huge grainy bulk and breaks it with precision. Holding the cheese over the scales positioned on top of the refrigerator case, Mario glances up now and then to make sure of my undivided attention. Deliberately lowering his hand slowly, he places the wedged morsel on the tray. His eyes dance back and forth from me to the finely marked numbers on the scales. The moment of truth arrives as the finely pointed needle stops and registers exactly un etto, instantly he gives a pride-filled, orgasmic grunt and thrusts his fist into the air shouting, *"É perfetto, no?"* (Is perfect, no?)

Laughing at his uninhibited performance, I agree, *"Perfetto, sì."*

The machine noisily executes its service of grating the cheese, and Mario tears off a piece of white waxed paper from a large roll. He folds and tears again the desired size from the end. With not a millimeter of waste he dumps the grated particles in the center, folds it in half, and crumples the three sides together. Giving the little homemade package to Beatrice and displaying an air of satisfaction, he proudly announces his latest sale. *"Un etto di parmigiano, sono quattro mila."* (One-fourth pound of cheese is $3.) She mimics his parlance, rhythmically punching the amount into the register.

17

They smile at me fumbling in my purse to find the correct amount of change among the unfamiliar currency. Oh, everything takes so much time now. Nothing is easy anymore. Beatrice puts the purchase in a used plastic bag advertising another shop's name and address.

Looking up to the shop's high, vaulted cathedral ceiling, "*É bellisima*" (It is beautiful), I say to Beatrice.

The owner nods in agreement. "*Sì, secolo diciassettesimo. Lei é Tedesca?*" (Seventeenth century. Are you German?)

"No."

"*Inglese?*" (English?)

"No, *Io sono Americana.*"

"*Ah, brava!*"

The acceptance warms me and I express my thanks. "Grazie, Signora."

"*Ah, grazie mille, signora Americana, e buon giorno.*" (A thousand thanks. Good day.)

"Buon giorno," I respond and step onto the busy street.

I have no choice but to repeat the same course home. I am consumed with thoughts of the farcical interlude, reflecting on the little dance sequence with Mario while he and Beatrice shouted conjectures of various food products at me. It brings a smile to my lips. Who knows, with the right catchy music, we could probably develop a new dance craze based on that frolic.

Two very basic things are different between the Italian and American cultures -- one, the insensitive encroachment Italians take of an American's private range of ease, and two, "*Io non capisco*" doesn't mean "I don't understand," as we were taught by Concetta in language class; it really means, "please talk loudly!"

Delighting in the scenario, I glance up from the stone street which my eyes have followed since leaving the delicatessen. I realize I am under close scrutiny by a petite woman who is wearing black from the soles of her feet to her

Front of our house number 24.

tiny little neck. The woman is taking wilted carnations from a container fastened to the wall of the house and positioned under a round, framed picture of the Madonna holding the Christ child. She is distracted from her duties by my presence and absentmindedly drops the fresh bouquet into the vase at a lopsided angle, whereupon a harsh and clamorous reprimand is heard as another little feminine wisp appears in a duplicating black garb. Seizing the project and rescuing the cockeyed bouquet, she arranges it to her satisfaction. Stepping back to give her finished work an approving nod, she crosses herself, paying homage to the image. Turning slightly, she smiles at me. "Buon giorno, Signora."

"Buon giorno," I respond, coupled with a friendly smile. The clone imitates the greeting, and they enter the French doors next to my security gate.

At least the neighbors are friendly, I think, while gazing at the front of my strikingly attractive white stucco house with the hunter green trim on the gate and on the French doors above, behind a three-foot-high iron railing. Pink-vined geraniums would be a nice accent up there, spilling over against the white background of the house.

Suddenly I feel I'm not alone and turn to the left, my eyes fall on the two flower arrangers who are standing in their doorway studying me. I smile and nod at the duo leaving them behind to find another source of entertainment.

Entering the porte-co-chere, I admire the arched stone canopy above which provides shelter for the metal clothes rack on the left side wall. It is ladened with freshly done intimate laundry of both sexes. I can't help thinking how curious it is to put one's underwear on public display. There is a blue motor scooter on my right, opposite the rack.

Unbeknownst to Gaines and I, our little corner of the world is under continuous reconnaissance. Nothing escapes the surveillance of Antonia Sebastiani, the erstwhile flower arranger known by all as "the Signorina"; her slightly younger and pliable sibling, Gabriella, is a widow and has returned to her birthplace

Stone stairs with moss stains.

to share life and expenses with the Signorina. Often they are joined by Lucia Mocavero, also a widow of septuagenarian status wearing the identical color, style, and curious, searching expression of the sisters. She lives next door to them, but upstairs.

If the threesome aren't keeping a neighborhood watch from the front window or Lucia's second story balcony, they are making the rounds of Via dei Sepolcri Messapici at a snail's pace, walking arm-in-arm, robed in the traditional garments of mourning--questioning, surveying, and surmising the affairs of all. No human or any other living being escapes the notice of their judgmental monitoring.

Undertaking the steep climb of the outside stairs, I am hit with a pang of lonely uneasiness which is symbolically matched by the unsightly moss stains facing me on each step. Willfully pushing the ill feelings of not belonging and what in the world are we doing over here back to where they reared their ugly heads, I leave all unpleasantness behind and take on the needs and demands of the rest of the day by emptying the luggage, organizing closets and drawers.

The neighborhood sounds keep me company as I work. The ladies are returning from marketing and wishing one another "Buon appetito" as they part company and return to their kitchens to put finishing touches on the main meal of the day. By one-thirty all of the outside activities have been put to rest for a few hours while the natives enjoy *il pranzo* (the noonday meal) consisting of at least three courses and leads almost everyone to their bed chambers for a lovely nap, riposo.

The company keeps an American schedule, so I don't expect Gaines home for hours. I gaze out on the sunlit, vacant street where the only evidence of life is a scroungy cat in search of a benevolent handout. The uneasiness tries to surface again, but I will it back, hoping to bury it forever. I take my Italian dictionary, pen and notebook to the dining room table. It has green, rose, and yellow marble inlaid in the light grey background. I trace the design with my finger and realize how

Dining room and view into living room.

cold marble can be. I begin to look up necessary words such as *dentifricio, carta igienica* and *sapone* (toothpaste, toilet paper, and soap) and practice saying each one aloud trying to get used to hearing myself say them in privacy, hoping to master the sounds so Mario and Beatrice can understand me the next time I go to the store.

Gaines' footsteps are followed by the banging door. The noise of his wingtips make a reverberating sound as he comes down the long, narrow hallway. He flings his soft cowhide briefcase on to the kitchen table as he passes the large arched opening to the set-aside area, falters on the three inch step down into the spacious, light-filled dining room, and looks down at the narrow ledge. "Hum, I'm going to have to get used to that!" I look up at him and smile as I'm still seated at the table working on my list of words.

"I got our car this morning," he announces with excitement. "Whew," he continues, while dragging his hand across his brow. "Going around that obelisk down there at Porta Napoli is insane. All those drivers coming at you from all sides." He shakes his head, giving his body a shudder.

"You drove home all by yourself?" I ask in alarm. "You're not only brave, but mighty lucky."

"Stupid is more like it!" he responds. "Stupid for coming over here."

Taking a three by five card from his breast pocket and raising his eyebrows, he refers to the list on the card. "We all have to have our pictures taken for documents, and we have to go to the police station, it's called a *Questura*, to be registered for a *Permesso di Soggiorno* (permit to stay in Italy), and it has to be renewed in two years." Displaying annoyance, he continues, "We can't open a bank account just yet. I was informed this morning that we have to have work visas first. That's called a *Permesso di Lavoro*" (permit to work in Italy). Closing his eyes, he draws a deep breath, followed by controlled exhalation through his puffed-up cheeks. "And that has to be done in Chicago of all places!" Flinging his arms into the air, he

24

continues, "We've just been gettin' ready to come over here for the past six months. Wouldn't you think that they would have thought about that while we were over there?"

"Don't tell me you have to return to the States?"

"No, the company is supposed to handle it for us."

"What are we going to do with all that money we brought with us?"

Shaking his head he says, "We'll just have to carry it in our passport pouches around our necks and pray no one steals it."

"Our winter clothes should camouflage the bulkiness of the pouches."

"Well, we can't hide it in the house, that's for sure." Motioning with his hand, he says, "We don't know who lives around here."

"Or under us for that matter." Displaying an impish grin, I ask, "Did you notice their undies in the entrance, drying right out in view of the street?"

Shaking his head with laughter, "Sì, sì."

Rising, I notice the unsteadiness of the chair. Examining it and its mate, I find both quite rickety. "I love these chairs, but neither one is sturdy enough to use. Don't use them, Honey, until they are repaired. I want to see our new car, and besides, it's time for Bridgie to go out again."

"I couldn't find a parking space out in front, not that there would be room anyway, but I did find space down the street across from where our driver almost wiped out the man working on the table last night."

"Oh, don't remind me of that crazy fool. I get upset every time I think of him."

We walk about forty-five meters to the new car. "It's called a Croma," he says pointing to it.

"It's beautiful!"

"Yes, but impractical for us in the old city. I really wish they had given me a smaller and less conspicuous one."

25

Bridget shows her interest and takes care to smell each tire, circling the new acquisition. We return to the *cortile*, the French doors of the ground floor apartment open, and a man steps outside. Observing our entrance, he extends his hand to us and says, "Salvatore Pascarella, but call me Totó." He speaks in English, and stoops to stroke Bridget under her chin. "And who might you be?"

"She is Bridget, and we are Adrianne and Gaines Grant from the States."

"Glad to know you both. Stop here for a cup of caffé," Totó urges. "Come on, just for a little while, like."

"Okay!" We accept.

"The dog, she is welcome as well," he says, holding the door open for us.

We enter a large room with a vaulted ceiling. The furnishings are a hodgepodge. A bamboo settee is against the right wall and two matching chairs with faded chintz cushions are set at a right angle to it. A rattan coffee table rests in the center of the arrangement. In the far left corner a large screened television faces the entrance, and a single-sized iron daybed is positioned against the left side wall, comfortable for watching the tube. A coat rack is fastened to the outside wall between the entrance and a doorway leading into a large bedroom. Framed photographs are displayed with an assortment of bric-a-brac on whatnot shelves a meter and a half from the foot of the daybed. Mirrors exhibiting liquor labels are randomly hung on the dingy, off-white walls completing the decor.

We sit on the bamboo chairs and Bridget, still on the lead, eases herself down on the slippery marble flooring beside Gaines. "Lying down is the easy part; getting up is where you need to develop your skills," Gaines says to Bridget while looking at his host, who has positioned himself on the edge of the daybed. He lights a cigarette and takes a long drag, smiling at the dog admiringly.

"I notice you speak with an English accent. Have you spent much time in England?" Gaines asks.

"Yes, you see it was like this. I went to England after the war, like, to the Birmingham area. I worked in the mines for fifteen years and then in the textile mills until two years ago. I took me retirement and moved back to my parents house. My mother sold the top two floors after my dad died, and all eight of us kids was gone." Totó is of short stature but has a strong build and is used to a lot of hard work. He starts to chuckle, "When I went to England, they claimed they had won the bloody war, but it sure didn't seem like it to me. Everything was rationed and a person couldn't get anything decent to eat."

A large girl enters the room carrying a tray with caffettiera, sugar bowl, demitasse cups and saucers and tiny spoons. She smiles and speaks, "Hello, I am Stefania." She has a beautiful English accent.

"Yes, this is me daughter, like. Me wife isn't here because she is to have surgery in the morning."

Stefania is sixteen and has a very pretty face as well as a pleasing countenance. She has blue eyes and soft brown hair. When she speaks, she possesses all of the confidence of Margaret Thatcher. She pours and serves the caffé. Father and daughter toss the piping hot beverage down their throats in two quick swigs and sit looking amused at our inexperience. We are still trying to pick up the blistering hot cup handles, not having begun to taste the scalding brew.

Totó prophesies, "Oh, you'll get the hang of it after you've been here a while and drink it every day, like."

As we start up the stairs, Totó is standing in his doorway, hands in his trouser pockets, feet shod in white Dr. Scholl's sandals contrasted by brown silky socks, making a curious fashion statement. A cigarette dangles from his mouth, not bothering to remove it, he cocks his head as far back as possible in an effort to give his eyes some relief from the emitting pollution. "I'll walk the dog for you." We turn to thank him when he mischievously giggles and adds, "For a price!" Without committing ourselves, we agree to get to know Totó a little better before making any deals with him. Back at the apartment,

27

Gaines opens a bottle of water with a brass boot-shaped opener brought from home. I take two glasses from a glass-paneled china cabinet.

"Whew, I've got to dilute their brew. That's called mainlining on caffeine!" He takes another swallow and leans against the marble-topped counter, crossing his ankles. "This morning I paid two hundred thousand lire for a telephone deposit. The company is supposed to take care of it for us. Now, with today's exchange rate, that's about a hundred and eighty bucks."

"Wonderful, when will it be installed?"

"They didn't tell that!" Looking into the half-full glass, "That's another thing, we have to find out where to buy our drinking water. It may be that we can have it delivered."

My attention is distracted, and turning my head toward the living room. "Listen, sounds like something rustling in the trees out back." Setting my glass down, I start toward the living room, walking past Bridget sprawled on the dining room floor. Never one to be left out, but with much difficulty she starts to raise herself from the polished marble floor. I stoop to give her a hand. "You poor darling. These floors are terrible for you." We move toward the window at the end of the living room. Looking outside, I immediately step back from view. Laughing, I whisper, "Come here, Gaines. You've got to see this!"

"What is it?"

I motion him on and caution, "Don't let him see you."

He takes a quick look and shares my amusement. Together we steal another peek. Totó is standing on his flat-topped kitchen roof just below our living room window. He is holding a very long two-inch wooden strip which has a rusty tin can fastened to it by its flipped-back lid. The makeshift apparatus enables him to lift oranges from the neighbor's trees. He can get two in the can at once.

Darkness falls and I begin closing all the outside shutters. In the bath, just off the living room, and an easy reach from

28

Totó's kitchen rooftop, I find a gift plate of freshly picked oranges on the window sill outside.

"I wonder if the neighbor has given approval to Totó's activity?"

"*Chi sa*" (Who knows), Gaines says as he lifts one off the plate. "You want a slice?"

"Sì, sì."

4

The next morning is Friday, and I take stock of our dwindling food supply. After making a list for the weekend, I prepare to leave the house for my first shopping trip. "Gaines, I'm going up to have another dance with Mario."

"Fine, but look out for those large cans of olive oil!"

I walk through the courtyard with Bridget, who insists on a joint venture this morning. Reaching up to push the gate release located on the stone wall before entering the porte-cochére, I hear it click open. Assuming Gaines had released it, I turn to wave to him, but rather notice the resident orange fisherman coming outside, realizing that Totó has disengaged the lock.

He's wearing a wide-brimmed felt hat reminiscent of Bogart in a 1940s movie and an olive drab British army sweater outside his wool slacks. Brown leather, laced shoes have replaced the Dr. Scholl sandals. He can look rather decent when he wants to.

Walking toward me with a cigarette, which is rarely absent, dangling on the side of his mouth, he reaches out, takes the dog's lead from my hand and says, "Let's go!"

"What? You have a lot of nerve."

"You'll see," is the cocky response, said over his shoulder, as he and Bridget go out of the gate together.

"I hope I don't live to regret this," I murmur, as I hurry to catch up with them. He directs us to an open area which is a school yard two minutes from the house.

"Now," Totó informs me, "she," pointing to Bridget, "can do her business here. It's easy to get to, and it won't upset the neighbors, like." Totó guides me through the confusing streets

30

drawing my attention to signposts, markers, and various symbols that I can use as aids for a safe and unharassed return to the walls of home and security.

I'm grateful to him for his thoughtfulness but reflect on the boorish way he initiated his little tour this morning.

"Totó, when was that house built? It is awesome." He displays a total lack of interest and responds, "I dunno."

"Well, what kind of architecture is it?"

"Who knows."

Obviously he's no culture freak. I'll have to find another source to feed my aesthetic needs.

*

This evening the remainder of the Americans arrive in Italy and are met by those of us who have all of two days more of this foreign experience. On a previous visit Chet and Margie Robson rented a villa near the sea. It was the same time we found our apartment in *centro storico* (historic district). It was last October 28 when Margie and I found exactly where each of us wanted to live. I wanted to be in the heart of the historic district and she wanted the sea.

Margie's villa is in the small vacation community of San Cataldo, which is six kilometers from Lecce and within walking distance of the sandy beach on the Adriatic. The area is used by the natives for a summer vacation and weekend retreat from life in the city. They would never think of living out there on a full-time basis. To an American it isn't too far out of town to commute, but to an Italian it is unthinkable. They shake their heads and cluck their tongues when Margie informs them where she resides.

Numerous white stucco, two story condos dot the one lane drive which randomly weaves its way under densely populated trees of pine, acacia, laurel, and palm. Bougainvillea and wisteria are overtaking the place, but in the right spot one can catch a glimpse of the sea.

Bobby Gregory plans his entire three year's residence at the Hotel Tiziano.

5

Fine di Settimana (the weekend). Saturday is received with joy because Gaines is home for two days, and this time allows us to relax and to make discoveries of our new life. A free day is necessary for recovery, restoration and renewing of the psyche which is bruised and maimed from our arduous week.

The sun is warm and it is jacket weather. We close the gate and walk through the dirty stone passages layered with grime. The street sweeper's broom is a poor attempt and it makes one wish for a good hard rain to wash away the filth. We come to the Duomo Bar, where the aroma of the excellently roasted and brewed Italian caffé strays into the street with a whiff of chocolate, inviting passersby to enter for a fortifying lift. Even though we are inexperienced Italian caffé drinkers, the aroma lassos us and we are led inside with no free will of our own.

A waiter carries a large tray out of a swinging door and rests it on the bar. It is stocked with glistening, plump, hot brioche. I perceive Gaines' question and say, "Yes, I do want one." He orders caffé for me and cappucino for himself at the bar.

I look at the surroundings and select a small, round table draped with a heavy, white cotton twill cloth. Dark bentwood chairs are used at less than a dozen tables. Gaines brings our breakfast on a tray. We linger at the table admiring the restored, original stones that have been stripped to their natural beauty on the magnificently constructed vaulted ceiling. Painted white walls complement the aging, yellowing, petrified lining arched above. New marble flooring and mahogany cabinetry are reflected in the beveled mirrors, enhancing the setting.

Unlike us, the natives rush in, hug the bar, gulp the scalding potion in a couple of swallows, and devour a small pastry while juggling a cigarette, purse (men's or women's), a morning paper, and oftentimes a car radio which is removed as a precautionary measure when one abandons their vehicle. To our amazement, all of the paraphernalia is of no hindrance to the social activity of brushing cheeks, puckering in mid-air, and rapid chit-chat. Italians are not quiet people and it is always noisy where they congregate. Daily devotion to this abbreviated exercise is accomplished in three to five minutes, followed by a fast-paced exit, because, wherever it is that they are going, they should have been there at least thirty minutes earlier. With a bit of envy, I look at people conversing because I can't communicate yet and it makes me long to speak their language.

After caffé there are errands of one sort or another. On this first Saturday, a *blocca-sterzo* has been suggested as a wise investment, so it is purchased at Standa. The three-quarter-inch round, steel, telescoping device displays a hook on each end. Gaines loops one end around the brake. Holding it upright, he inserts the other end while pushing the two pieces together until the top hook clasps around the steering wheel. It is locked in the center by a key. This trusty little invention holds the steering wheel tightly in place and gives the owner a sense of security against the many bands of notorious car thieves. Gaines locks the car, and looking inside he expresses his confidence. "That ought to discourage anyone from trying to steal it!" The car is left locked and safe from thieves.

Feeling exhausted from fighting traffic, crowds, and people in so-called lines who shove one another this way and that in order to accomplish everything before the town folds up for the midday pause, we wearily approach our front gate. Totó appears out of nowhere on his only means of transportation, the little blue scooter. Greeting us with an impish grin, he takes notice of our shopping bags from Standa (the K-Mart of Italy) remarking, "That's a bloody expensive place to shop!"

33

I feel it is none of his business and ignore the caustic comment. "How is your wife, Totó? Is she getting along okay after surgery?"

Removing his cigarette and flicking the accumulation of ash particles, "She's going to have it Monday, like," he informs us while pushing his scooter inside the gate. He positions it in the porte-co-chére next to the right wall, in front of the miniature-sized door which leads to a small room under the stairs. A small recessed window is above the bike. I try unsuccessfully to see into the area when I'm drawn back by Totó, who is taking lumpy plastic bags from his handlebars.

"This morning I was able to get some nice greens, *cicoria*" (chicory).

The comment ignites a famished Gaines. "What's for lunch, anyway?"

My energy is sapped from the strenuous morning, and I am not able to address that issue yet.

"Totó, where do you go for a good plate of pasta around here, nearby ?"

"I'm tellin' you, Signora, I wouldn't pay anyone to feed me!"

"Really?" I smile at him thinking, you are cocky!

*

It is Sunday and it has always been our habit to be in church. Nothing will change now because we have relocated to a foreign country. There are four protestant groups represented in Lecce, a city of one-hundred-thousand people, Christian, Pentecostal Christians, Jehovah Witness and Mormon. The number of protestants in Italy is very small compared to those of the Catholic faith. We will attend The Christian Church of Lecce, because its doctrine is much the same as ours at home.

"Do you know how to get there?" I ask, in an amusing tone.

Chuckling at our predicament. "I believe so, and I think we ought to leave the car parked where it is," Gaines suggests.

"I want to walk!" I pick up my coat and hand it to Gaines. "It will help us familiarize ourselves with the area."

"There really isn't any sense in taking the car." He places my coat on my shoulders and commences to list his reasons with the aid of his fingers. "By the time we walk to the car, fool with the blocca-sterzo, find the best route out of the quarter and to church, secure a parking place there because there's no parking lot, and put the blocca-sterzo back on the car, it will take us at least twenty minutes--maybe more!"

"You don't have to convince me!"

We pass groups of black-garbed ladies on their way to Mass. It has been said by Catholic friends that many Italians have fallen away from regular attendance in recent years and the Mass draws more of the elderly than any other group.

The church we are going to was founded thirty-six years ago by an American couple from Ohio. They have raised three boys and a daughter in Lecce. The pastor died a few months ago and the new minister is an Italian who grew up in the church and went to a seminary in Florence. Everyone is very friendly giving the Italian cheek-to-cheek greeting, hugging us in a boisterous fashion and wishing us, *buona Domenica*. (Have a good Sunday.) A few can speak English and interpret, thus softening the confusion for us. Gaines, not used to being kissed by the brethren, has to rescue his glasses every now and then as they get knocked from side to side by the zealots in their show of acceptance. The order of the service and the songs is familiar to us, but it is in Italian.

We stroll home and I admire a flower shop which is doing a good business from some who want a bouquet to take to a hostess for dinner and others who are visiting the cemetery.

"Let's stop for a cup of caffé," I suggest. The bar is full of people buying pastries too pretty to eat. The clerks put the chosen morsels on heavy paper trays and wrap them in paper advertising the name and address of the bar. The package is tied up with ribbon.

35

We are preoccupied with all the newness that has invaded our lives and do not converse while drinking the brew. We have to stand at the counter because there are no tables and chairs in this bar.

Gaines buys *La Republica*, a newspaper from Rome at the *edicola* (newsstand) beside the old city gate of Rudiae. We walk through the arched entrance of the gate, holding our breath against the ammonia stench of urine remaining in the path basin of centuries-worn marble. Unfortunately, some people relieve themselves in public.

"It is impossible not to step in it," I say, with disgust.

We pass the Church of the Holy Rosary, dedicated to St. John the Baptist. It took 37 years to build this Baroque church in the late seventeenth century, according to the restorer's sign. Its beautiful decoration is hidden under scaffolding and the interior is locked to the public while under restoration. There is a crane at the sight with a huge concrete block suspended high over the street. It gives me a feeling of uneasiness as we walk under it. "Isn't it strange to leave that block up there like that? I hate to walk under it!" Gaines laughs and takes my hand.

Most of the houses and buildings lining the street are of the Baroque period. "Oh, Gaines, I love this street and I want to know about the buildings and the original purpose of each one."

"The architecture doesn't stir me in the way it does you, Adrianne, but what I like is the fact that Sunday is like it used to be at home. Only a few places open for business. It feels quiet and restful. A day for church and family."

Fifty yards from Holy Rosary Church, we look inside the smaller Church of St. Ann, also late seventeenth century. It is uninspired architecturally, not as ornate or elaborate as most of the churches of Lecce, but its plain statement says there is beauty in simplicity. The height of the wooden ceiling is awesome.

A few meters more in the same block as the other two churches is the former Convent of the *Scalzi Carmelitani* (bare-footed, Carmelite Nuns). They were barefoot, a requirement in taking a vow of poverty. It is adjacent to St. Teresa Church

(1626-27). The main door of the church is basically Renaissance in style. Over the portal is a large window that was rebuilt in the middle of the nineteenth century but still has the lines of the eighteenth century, the remaining architecture is Baroque.

We turn left, walking past the side of Mario's Salumeria and meander down Sepolcri Messapici where the children are outside playing soccer in our narrow street.

When we arrive at the gate, Gaines' key is aimed and prepared for manipulating the lock, but we hear the familiar click and realize it has been triggered from the inside by our neighbor who steps outside bearing the usual curious eye of surveillance. Totó deduces our mission has been one of a spiritual nature this Sunday morning and deems it necessary to comment.

"I don't go to church meself. I've no use for them money grubbin' priests. All they wants is to get their bloody hands in your pockets, and most of them goes to the prostitutes."

"Go with us next Sunday." I smile.

"Oh, no! Thanks just the same. I'm not interested. Send the dog down and I'll take her out."

"Thanks, Totó," I reply.

Gaines shuts the door. "Smelling his food makes me hungry. Wish we were invited."

Il nido, our nest.

6

The beginning of my first week here feels strange. I realize that I can't live here as I did at home and nothing is the same anymore. I must start to blend in and learn how to live as a native. So I set out on this Monday morning to buy fresh bread and shop for the day. It is easy because I can walk everywhere I need to go and it becomes an adventure. I meet my neighbors out in the street and we attempt to converse but it is difficult and tiring. By the time I find my way back to the house and have lunch, I'm exhausted and feel the need to retreat to *il nostro nido* (our nest) for riposo. It is the family room, a snuggery, a cozy place at the top of the dining room stairs sandwiched between the master bedroom and a small boudoir that I use for ironing as well as dressing.

A bamboo-framed sofa, which in a pinch can be used as an extra bed, is placed next to the decorative white iron rail bordering the stairwell. It faces a massive smooth-surfaced stone fireplace protruding into the room. A stone hearth ledge approximately a foot high surrounds the three exposed sides. The mantle duplicates these lines and the chimney tapers slightly as it converges to the ceiling. A panel of Baroque sculpted scrolls, arabesques, and filigree had been placed between the mantle and the hearth by the contractor-restorer, Maestro Franco Pietro.

A television rests on a stone bench built next to the fireplace. Light filters in from the long, paneled windows of the French doors high above the courtyard. Bridget and I rest together in il nido on the sofa which is long and comfortable.

Suddenly I am awakened and stricken with disbelief that it is already dark. Flipping on the light and checking my watch, I

One view of Sepolcri Messapici,
from our gate to the furniture shop.

discover that Gaines will be home soon. Bridget, in slow motion, is stretching her long, red, front legs downward to the highly polished floor, displaying a little stiffness as she scoots from her resting place.

"Let's go meet Daddy." The suggestion gives a boost to her energy and the *quattro zampe* (four-legged animal) nimbly takes to the staircase. Her tail is up and swishing like a rust-colored flag.

Proceeding to the dimly lit courtyard, I notice Totó's front room is a hive of activity. The uninhibited card players can be heard into the street. At evenly spaced intervals decorative, oversized, black, wrought iron coach lights jut from the stone houses on ornamental arms and provide brightness throughout the quarter.

We stroll toward the illuminated furniture shop. Pasquale Bianco and his son, Maurizo, are out in front of their establishment stripping the finish from a large armoire. The project doesn't leave ample space for motorists to negotiate the limited twisting turns of the sidewalk free passageway known as Via dei Sepolcri Messapici.

When translated the street name means tombs of the Messapici. The Messapici race were ancient people who came to the territory from what is known today as Albania. They settled in Lecce and the region of Puglia before Christ. Every time one of the utility companies deems it necessary to lift the stones and make adjustments of one sort or another under the streets, their remains are uncovered.

I pause to admire the fine old mahogany furniture when my attention is enticed to a sight of quite another sort. My eyes follow the two scantily dressed spectacles, obviously outfitted for their particular line of work, coming from the other side of the shop. At that moment I see Gaines coming and motion to him of their departure so he can get their parking space.

"Signora, signora."

I turn to see a familiar face confronting me from the opened French doors. The sixtyish woman is Isabella Carlucci

41

and she is not bestowing friendliness or goodwill toward me. She directs my attention to quattro zampe, who has done her "business" under the woman's doors while my attention was drawn elsewhere.

"Oh, *scusa, scusa, me dispiace.*" (Excuse me, I'm sorry.) Quickly I take a plastic bag from my coat pocket and by pushing a gloved hand deep down inside, I pick up the excrement and invert the bag by pulling the opening over the fully protected hand.

Isabella is still agitated, and holding her nose yells, "*Puzzo,puzzo*" (stink) at me and Bridgie.

I step across the tiny passage way and deposit the bag in a dumpster.

Pasquale gives us a nasty look and then he yells, "*Vai,via*" (go away), waving his hand in the opposite direction.

"We're not making friends, Bridget."

Gaines emerges from the car with a scowl on his face.

"Is he mad at us, too?" Bridget is not deterred and lunges toward him breaking her tie with me. Bridget pushes her nose into Gaines' thighs, wagging her entire back side excessively. Picking up her lead, Gaines takes Bridgie around the car. I trace their path and discover the reason for his grimaced expression when I'm faced with the long, deep scratch along the door of our beautiful new car.

"How did it happen?"

"Oh, it's my fault, aiming for their parking place, not allowing enough space back there at the Baron's Palazzo. I scraped the car on his concrete planter. Why is he allowed to stick it out there in the way? How can he get away with that?"

"Probably because he's titled!"

I spy a familiar face approaching us. He is walking beside a bicycle this evening. Sometimes he carries a tire or some other bike part. His demeanor suggests he is on an errand. His clothes are always jeans and a pullover. His physique and agility suggest a middle-aged adult, but when confronted by the piercing blue eyes encircled by deep lines, his septuagenarian

42

status is betrayed. He is a striking old pet with his leathery-toned skin and thick crop of remaining snow-white hair fashioned in a 1950s flat-top, crew-cut style.

The previous evening I met him not for the first time and decided to speak. I mistakenly said, "Buon giorno" (Good day), when every Leccese knows that after five o'clock the greeting changes to *buona sera* (good evening).

He returned my mistaken greeting with a haughty reprimand and responded, "Hum, buona sera!" It was said very curtly and left me humiliated and put down. I decide not to be outdone by him this evening and when he comes close to us, I say, "Buona sera," with such exaggeration that Gaines looks down at me bewildered.

This act brings a smile to the old man's lips and he returns the greeting, asking me. "*Loro sono Tedesce?*" (Are you all German?)

"No."

"Inglese?"

"No, *siamo Americani.*"

"Oh, *bravi, bravi!*" He exudes much warmth toward us and then he says in English. "Youa wanta somsing tua eata boy?" Throwing his head back with hearty laughter, he is pleased to be able to say something to us in our native tongue.

"Our GIs of World War II," comments Gaines. "Bless them, he has never forgotten." We smile at each other and at him full of pride.

Then the old gentleman begins to sing, "Pistol Packin' Mama."

We were small children when the song was a popular tune and remember hearing it on the radio.

"*Come si chiami?*" (What are your names?)

"Gaines and Adrianne Grant."

"*Piacere.*" (Pleased to meet you.)

"*Come si chiama?*" (What is your name?) Gaines asks.

"*Io sono Antonio, ma i miei amici mi chiamano Uccio.*" (I am Antonio but my friends call me Uccio. Uccio is the Italian

43

nickname for Antonio, not Tony, which is an anglicized version of Antonio.)

We say goodbye to Uccio and start toward the gate. I look up to the back side of the parallelogram-shaped, two-story furniture shop to the little balcony with two clothes lines conveniently placed for freshly done hand wash.

"Everyday the most beautiful lingerie hangs on those lines, Gaines. I've never seen such beautiful undergarments in my life, and everyday there is a different color hanging up there!"

"Business must be good."

7

As each day passes, Totó is integrating himself into our private lives, regardless of whether we want his attention or not. He seems to be "Johnny on the Spot" at every opportune moment, offering his services by querying, "Do you need hands?" Never waiting for a reply, he continues his mission of helpfulness, displaying a generous, benevolent nature as well as disguising his insatiable nosy streak. He carries grocery sacks, fetches the heavy plastic cartons containing a dozen glass bottles of drinking water, totes garbage bags to nearby dumpsters, and escorts Bridget on her necessary outings, giving a detailed report on their return: "she done her business, like," or "she had a bit of a wee."

Remaining true to his Italian nature, Totó wants to feed everything in sight except for the band of mangy neighborhood cats, which he only fed once! Bridget adores his little treats. She isn't too keen on him at first, but he plies her with tasty morsels the leftovers from his refined culinary skills.

She likes the treats much better than they do her; her delicate digestive system is in rebellion most of the time. I have already issued an explanation for my pet's disorder and naively think that my wishes of not feeding Bridget will be honored, especially since Totó looked me in the eye and nodded his head in agreement that Bridget shouldn't be fed from the table. However, evidence is soon discovered that man and dog have a secret alliance because she unceasingly betrays their dark business. I try to figure out how to deal with the Italian mentality. One Italian writer had written about it but had not given the reader a clue as to how to cope with the national disorder.

I am faced with a very serious expression as I open the door. Totó looses Bridget from the lead and she runs inside. "Oh, hi, Totó! Would you like to come in?"

He ignores my invitation and does not return my friendly greeting. Brushing it aside, he says, "What have you been feedin' the dog? She's bloody sick today!"

"What? It's not what I feed her, it's what you've been sneaking her that is the problem! Furthermore, don't bother to deny it because I have seen the evidence."

"I've been carin' for dogs all me life, and I've never hurt one yet!"

"Bridget is different. She cannot tolerate rich foods."

The only acknowledgment of his guilt is a deflated countenance. Weakly he says, "Send her down later and I'll take her out when I gets back from the hospital, like."

"Did your wife have her surgery?"

"No, them bloody doctors put it off again. I can't stand the sight of them." Waving his hands in the air, he starts down the stairs.

"Oh, Totó! There isn't a mailbox? Where does the postman put the mail?"

Holding to the handrail, he casually turns with an air of indifference saying, "Oh, he just tosses it in the cortile, like, or he might lay it on the back of the scooter. That's good enough no one's going to bother it."

"Really?" I'm going to have a mailbox, I think, as I close the door.

I look at my watch and at that moment, I hear Gaines shut the security gate. Being a creature of habit, Gaines leaves for the office at seven-thirty every morning Monday through Friday. He likes order and structure in his life, has little patience for tardiness, and does not allow impromptu activity to transpire very often. It is difficult to imagine this man managing and working with a people who love spontaneity and never allow an excess of order and discipline to hamper their impulsive lifestyle to the extent of it becoming a habit-forming practice. With

46

Gaines walking to the car.

Gaines' quotidian departure, Bridget and I stand in the open French doors of the guest room above the front gate and watch him walk down the old stone street until he unfailingly turns to wave goodbye before disappearing from sight.

Bridget has a cognizance of time and consistently marks the hour of Gaines' arrival. When his key enters the lock at seven-fifteen, her fervor is revved into a state of frenzy by the time he enters the front door. She unleashes a show of enthusiasm lasting all of thirty seconds. Gaines enters the kitchen, which is jokingly referred to as the chicken by us, because Italians studying English seem to confuse the two words. It is retaliation on our part for all of the humiliation suffered over our own language problems.

"Hi."

"Guess what? I found a parking space real close tonight and only had to drive around the area once!"

"Good for you. It is such a hassle for you every night." Bridget paws at Gaines and runs to the door, repeating the charade. "She just got home. Totó brought her in not more than five minutes ago."

Gaines looks at her winsome face and takes pity on her. "I'll take her out for a bit. We won't be gone long."

In a few minutes they return with Gaines shaking his head and looking very puzzled. "I think she wanted to know where the car is parked. She walked right to it, smelled all around the tires, and then looked at me as if to say I know where it is, now let's go home."

"The first thing you said tonight entering the chicken was, 'Guess what? I found a parking place real close.' Come to think of it, I believe that is the very first topic of conversation every night when you get home. She understands."

Bridget continues her nightly inspection as long as we have the Croma.

View of front gate from dining room.

8

I am reflecting on our first week in Lecce, as I start down the stairs with the breakfast tray. Suddenly that unsettling buzzer blasts simultaneously with my arrival on the last step into the dining room. Peering out of the French doors, I view Margie Robson at the front gate gazing up in my direction. Margie smiles upon seeing my face, waves and says "Hello" in her high-pitched, melodic tone that is idiosyncratic and seems to take flight above any other sound.

The annoying buzzer, as well as the familiar voice, awakens Bridget from her morning drowsiness all curled up in a sun splotch on the sofa in il nido. She scurries to the lower level with nails clicking on the marble stairs and slides on her hip as she tries to maneuver the right turn from the dining room into the hallway while groping to get some balance on the slippery floor. However, she makes it to the door just as I open it for my welcomed friend.

Margie is a tall, big-boned, heavyset lady in her mid-fifties. Her normal attire is jeans, sweatshirt, and running shoes. This morning she has not altered her style. Her jet black hair is pulled straight back, twisted into a knot on the back of her head, and held in place by a matching-colored, plastic, spiral cup pierced by a four inch blade. Glasses rest on her scrubbed, make-up-free face.

"Kid, I was drivin' up that Via Palmieri down there and I smelled donuts. I didn't think Eyetalians knew how to make um!" Pointing to her nose, she laughs, "It never fails me."

Leading down the hall, Margie turns right into the kitchen alcove. "I'll just set them here in the 'chicken.' " Then, she realizes she is going to have to scoot the box of goodies to the center of the square-shaped, wooden table out of the reach of the jaws and long red paws that are threatening the supply. "Can she have one?" Margie asks me in an affected, pleading manner.

Feigning disapproval, I prolong a drawn-out sigh. Yet I acquiesce and break the ring in half, placing it in the stainless steel bowl saying, "Buon appetito, Bridgie."

Pouring Margie a cup of freshly brewed coffee with hazelnut aroma, I implore my friend, "Well, why don't you put that nose to some really good use and sniff out some super-crunch peanut butter and cheddar cheese? I'm starting to go through withdrawal."

Margie takes another bite of the donut and before it has cleared her mouth, she offers, "Do you want to drive over to the market this morning?"

"Sure, but it's so close. Why don't we just walk over to it. The traffic is wild and crazy out there on those streets."

Margie wipes her hands on a paper napkin and as she takes a swipe at her mouth, declares. "Kid, if you can drive in Houston, you can drive anywhere!"

I consider the response with skepticism, but yield to the driver's notion. "Our personal belongings are to be delivered from Naples this morning, but I'll ask Totó to let the delivery in."

Bridget is left in the neighbor's care and we start out to drive to the market in Chet's new company car. We know where the market is, but driving there is another matter. It takes time to master traffic patterns and one-way streets in centro storico. We find ourselves facing oncoming vehicles more times than we are emotionally equipped to handle. The mid-morning traffic is heavy because natives are impatient to finalize shopping and errands before all commerce ceases for the midday break. The snarl of congestion is confusing, mentally draining and is downright life-threatening. The drivers yell, jeer, honk and give us gestures not resembling any sort of admiration.

"Adrianne, I think that all these Eyetalians are so hostile because of apartment living. Being pent up all of the time, they just get downright mean."

51

"You might be right. Oh, look! Let's take that street." I motion to a passage off the Piazza which we have inadvertently circled more times than we want to remember. To our disappointment, however, when we are more than halfway down the block we discover that the short street is barricaded. At that precise moment, a truck loaded with plastic cartons full of water bottles stacked several feet high, double parks on the right side of the street behind us. The driver springs from the cab, hoists a carton on his shoulder, and disappears into the bank.

With the aid of the side and rear-view mirrors, Margie continues to back very slowly between the truck and the multicolored border of cars on the left. Relief is only seconds away when another truck drives into the lane imitating the behavior of the first driver. The second one double parks on the left side, just a car's length from us to the end of the first truck. This driver also disappears for parts unknown and is oblivious to the chaos he has created. Margie quickly cuts to the right and backs between the rear end of truck number one on her right front and the rear left side of truck number two, skillfully clearing all metal surrounding them. Three men idling on the corner are being entertained by this unplanned sequence of events.

"You're fine, Margie. You're going to make it!"

The macho threesome part company. One positions himself in front of the car and begins gesturing with raised hands, motioning toward the car in a synchronized action. The second individual finds his post in the rear. His directional movements are of *una staccata* nature and are coupled with a pantomime of turning the steering wheel while emphatically yelling, "*Dai, dai* (pronounced die but means come on), Signora."

Somewhat annoyed at their belated and unsolicited assistance, I ask. "What, pray tell, does *dai, dai* mean anyway?"

"Gosh, I don't know. But I wish the critters that caused us this trouble would!"

Abruptly, two huge, muscular, hairy arms are thrust through the driver's open window and attach massive hands to the steering wheel replacing Margie's. To her astonishment, she is silenced, suffering from his jabbing right elbow, but she is cooperative and continues to execute her feet through appropriate movements on the brake, clutch, and accelerator. The pedestrian driver takes his mission much too seriously, gyrating the steering wheel and escorting us out of the small street into the Piazza. He continues to accompany the freed vehicle giving everyone in the area an opportunity to take notice of his chivalrous act.

Joining him at the driver's window are his cronies and it is as if a euphoric spell is cast on all five of us beings of on-the-spot acquaintanceship, friendly inquiries are made followed by well-mannered and appreciative replies for the natives' samaritanism. Laughter and gaiety is present and accompanied by numerous grazies, buon giornos, and ciaos.

The amusement of spontaneous diversion was sought this morning. Margie and I set out to find it at the market, buying little trinkets to take home, but our fun is found on an ordinary street just off the Piazza. The curious mishap brings pleasure every time it surfaces in our memories.

*

It is not taking me as long to fuse into my new lifestyle as I thought it would. After an adventure with Margie this morning and the ordeal of buying the daily food supply followed by a light lunch, the sofa in il nido beckons.

Sounds of Lecce coming to life once more arouse me from drowsiness and luxuriating in a languid state, I am jolted out of my relaxation by the sound of the grating buzzer.

"Oh, who in the world?" I groan. Giving up the snuggery, I grudgingly go down the stairs and look out the French doors of the dining room. Fernanda Santini and Alessandra Grimaldi are waving to me. I push the gate release and step on to the balcony to greet the two visitors who are bustling through the courtyard.

"Buona sera, Adriana," they say, smiling up at me.

I hurry to the front door and am the recipient of a bouquet of pink tulips, as well as kisses on both cheeks from each lady. The sisters-in-law move through the chain of rooms and sit down together on a sofa loveseat in the living room. I follow, volunteering to hang up their wraps, but the offer is rejected as their visit will be brief.

Fernanda owns the apartment, but resides in Bologna. In her mid-forties she maintains a slender figure for her short stature and carries herself with a grand forbearance of headship. Her petite form is forever laden with the best money can buy, and she promotes every expensive adornment and label for which snobs yearn. Her smart, short, brown haircut is highlighted with a popular mahogany rinse which nicely compliments her Latin skin tone. A throaty huskiness betrays a nicotine habit. She has an aloof, more sophisticated way about her than does Alessandra, who is married to Fernanda's brother, Giovanni. They own a shop in modern Lecce.

"Would you like caffé?"

Both women emphatically shake their heads no. "No, grazie. We've had too much already today," Alessandra responds and stretches out her hand feigning a shaky condition from caffeine excess.

"Tell me about it. Half a demitasse is about all I can handle so far."

I open a chest door and bring out a brown ceramic vase with green, pink, and yellow in the design. I place the pink bouquet in it, adjust the tulips a little saying, "Why, there are thirteen, not a dozen!"

"Yes," volunteers Alessandra. "An uneven number has better eye appeal than an even number."

"You Italians think of everything. Excuse me while I add some water."

I step into the bath just off the living room. Returning, I place the vase on the chest. "Thirteen is considered an unlucky number in the States, but I'm not superstitious. The flowers are beautiful in that vase, Fernanda. Where did you find it?"

"Seventeen is unlucky in Italy, and the vase came from Bologna. How do you and Gaines like living here in my apartment? É bella, no?" She asks in a boastful way.

"Oh, the apartment, é bella sì, but there are a few things I need to discuss with you."

"Tell me, how is living here different from Illinois?" Fernanda asks.

"We had a house there and a yard, as well as a two-car garage. Gaines is not used to looking for a parking place every night. It is affordable to operate a clothes dryer. In this climate it takes three days for knit underwear to dry thoroughly. It was my custom back home to shop once or twice a week. We use a lot of frozen items. I'm not used to shopping every day, but I think the benefits of eating fresh food are superior for our health needs. It's these things that we have to adjust to, but we can do it in time."

Fernanda says, "*Ah,si,si,si. Le Pesce fresca qui é molto buono.*" (The fresh fish here is very good.)

"What I really need to discuss with you is the condition of the dining room chairs. I'm afraid to use them in their rather unstable condition." I go into the dining room, return with one of the chairs, and place some weight on it to exhibit how rickety it is.

Fernanda's prideful, pleasing expression is replaced with sober indifference. She removes her tobacco paraphernalia and prepares for a smoke. "The chairs are one hundred twenty-five years old, perfect with the ten thousand dollar table, no?"

I realize that Fernanda's romantic notion of old has a greater priority than does usability. "There really aren't adequate reading lamps here either." I wait for a response.

"Aren't the rugs beautiful? Kilim, antique, of course." Fernanda gives a satisfied smile, admiring the one before her.

My amusement with this starry-eyed romantic is mixed with irritation, but I decide to try again. "We need a mailbox. *Il postino* just tosses the mail into the cortìle."

55

"Yes, you do! I'll have one sent to you soon. That no good bastardo downstairs can't keep his nasty hands off the mail. He examines every piece. He called my daughter un beetch! Lui non é buono, non é buono. (He is no good.) Don't have anything to do with him." She shakes her finger in my face. Fernanda's dislike of Totó is indisputable.

I close the door and sigh with relief at their departure. "How about us going out for a walk?" Bridget moves toward the door before I can utter *andiamo*. We reach the bottom step when Totó's door springs open causing me to flinch. "You startled me!" I say laughing.

Dramatically, Totó steps outside looking very grave and says, "I saw that bloody bitch come in here. Did she give you any trouble, like?"

I stifle my amusement at his display of histrionics, managing to shake my head no and start toward the gate. He steps into my path to share a little more of his scorn. "That bigheaded snob! Thinks she is better than anyone around here. How much is she chargin' ya for that place upstairs?" he asks, pointing upward with his thumb. His eyes flash. He hates Fernanda as much as she does him.

I ignore his prying question. "Bridgie and I are going to stretch our legs around the Duomo Piazza. We won't be gone long." He reaches inside, pushing the lock release for us. Without turning, I say thanks over my shoulder and give a wave with my free hand.

We walk briskly around the large square which is accented by elegant black, wrought iron double-armed coach lamp stands. The original cathedral was built in 1114, and the present structure underwent complete restoration between 1659 to1670. The Archbishop's palace is between the church and the seminary. All buildings are attached and make up two sides of the Duomo square. A door is ajar and the oval-topped portal provides a perfect frame for the ancient well centered in the seminary courtyard.

Across the piazza is a five-story bell tower. The identical levels lessen in size as they reach the top. I scrutinize its not-so-graceful design when I see Alessandra and Giovanni on their terrace waving and motioning for me to come up.

The Grimaldi's penthouse reflects their warm, gracious personalities. A small, wood-stained horse without rockers greets the guests in the foyer. Bridget and I are ushered into a cozy sitting room with a corner fireplace. I admire the antique, caned, Louis XIV dressing armchair by the hearth. The graceful little legs rise thirteen inches from the floor, making it most commodious for fire gazing.

"*Prendi caffé*, Adriana?"

"Sì, grazie."

Giovanni pulls to the side the cutwork inset, linen window treatment on brass rings, letting in the brilliant half-sized disappearing sun that bids its adieu for another day. "Come out on the terrace," he suggests.

I follow, admiring their view of the Duomo Piazza.

"The bougainvillaea is beautiful."

"Sì, fuchsia is my favorite color. I'm training it to the wall."

Alessandra brings the tray outside and is followed by their son.

"This is our son, Claudio. He loves American basketball."

"Do you play yourself?" I ask.

"Yes, I play with friends out at San Cataldo."

"Your English is very good. Have you been studying very long?"

"A few years."

"Thanks for the caffé." I place the cup and saucer on the tray, and look at my watch. "I must be leaving, as it will be time soon for you all to return to the shop for the evening trade. I'll call you next week, we would love to have you all visit."

After saying our goodbyes, Bridget and I walk out into the midst of lots of activity. People are out shopping, interrupting missions of errands to chat with friends and going into the bars for espresso and a dessert. Looking from the outside, the lifestyle deceptively appears to be trouble free.

I notice a shop with the *cartapesta* figures in the window. The craft is as old as the stone street I'm standing on. The papier-mâché clothes of the figures are designed with detail and painted. The sculpted hands and face are intricately made of clay and painted to look natural. The subjects are religious figures as well as the professional or peasant folk, and they are all sizes. I have been told by a native that it is a tradition to parade Mary, mother of Christ, through the streets for certain holy days, and many years ago the wooden statues were too burdensome to carry. So out of this need, some ingenious artisan made a frame for the body, molded straw around the frame and designed clothes out of wet paper and paste. After it dried, a sculpted head and hands were attached to the body and the figure was painted. The idea was so successful that many have learned how to do the cartapesta, and even today young people train for this as a profession.

9

Finalization of two major events at this address are realized. The shipment of personal belongings, such as extra bed and bath linens, our summer wardrobes, cutlery, tools, books, a portable radio-cassette player, tapes, shopping cart and a Bunn-o-Matic coffee maker arrives from Naples three weeks after we were told it would be delivered the next day.

Sofia has had her long-awaited hemorrhoid surgery and is now convalescing at home. She and Stefania share the same physical likeness nice features: soft brown hair, blue eyes and body type big. Sofia moves very slowly into the cortile to observe Totó, who is disassembling the packing crates. Standing motionless like a square box herself, she looks intently with her mouth ajar. They speak with such speed that I can't decipher a single word that is said. Two women enter the cortile through the partially opened gate. Sofia returns their friendly greetings, but Totó's attitude is inhospitable toward them.

Sofia introduces me to Domenica Toro. She is attractive, but a little bit of the middle-aged spread shows in her mid-section. Self-consciously, she tries to hide it with the use of a wool shawl wrapped around her shoulders and held in place by folded arms. "This is my daughter, Tiziana. She is to be married this summer."

"Piacere, Signora." Tiziana smiles and extends her large hand to me. Tiziana is head and shoulders taller as well as bulkier than anyone present.

I am reminded of the old adage she could go bear hunting with a switch. "Piacere, Tiziana."

Their conversation with Sofia doesn't sound like any Italian, I have ever heard before.

"Adriana, Domenica and Tiziana live next door. They will be happy to help you unpack and put things away if you like."

"Tell them thanks, but I can manage it."

Stefania enters the cortile. Bridgie runs to her and she stoops to give the dog a hug. "Ciao, Bella mia," she speaks to everyone, but gives me the cheek to cheek greeting, and the dog follows Stefania into the house.

Sofia takes a photo out of her apron pocket and shows it to me. "This is my little dog, Randy. He is still in England because it was too expensive to bring him with us."

"He is a Chihuahua. How cute! I know you must miss him terribly."

"Oh, sì, sì."

I notice a hint of an Irish accent when Sofia speaks English. Sofia brushes away a tear and gazes at the photo. She starts to cry openly and takes a handkerchief from her dress pocket blowing her nose loudly. I touch her shoulder. "Sofia, I'm sorry you couldn't bring Randy to Italy with you. I understand, I couldn't have stood to leave my dog. Maybe Bridgie can help you."

Totó puts a box marked appropriately in black ink on the kitchen table. He takes a knife from his front pocket and cuts the heavy-duty packing tape. "You know them two that was downstairs?"

"Are you referring to Domenica and Tiziana?"

"Ya, ya, them two. Well, I don't wants 'em up here, like. They're a bloody nuisance."

"Totó, I hope you never feel that way about me."

He grins at my remark. "Now, I'm not tryin' to interfere in your business, but just don't let them get started, like."

Ignoring his suggestion, I change to what I assume is a safe subject. "Did you and Sofia marry here or in England?"

Totó snaps his eyes at me, as if a fire has been ignited and feigns repulsion at the very idea. Indignantly he says, "I didn't marry her!"

"Well, excuse me! You've just been referring to her as 'me wife' for the past three weeks! What is a person supposed to think?"

He puts his hands together in a prayerlike position moving them in an up and down fashion. "I'll explain." Basking in the limelight, he begins. "It's like this. When I went to England, young fool that I was, I married the first girl I met because she got pregnant." He emphasizes she as if she had accomplished the feat all by herself. He begins to chuckle. "Her name was Joan Collins." I smile, as Totó continues. "She had five kids. One right after another. One day she called me a bloody Eyetie and I knocked her to the floor. Oh, the Judge fined me, made me pay some damages, like, but it was bloody worth it. I got so I couldn't stand her, so I left her and me five kids. I worked with Stefania's father and he died when she was just a baby. I started seeing Sofia. She's not very smart, but she is a good woman."

*

I lead Stefania, Sofia, Domenica and Tiziana into the living room. It is the third afternoon this week that the quartet has come to visit after riposo. I really don't mind, as my days are terribly long and the visits help to get better acquainted. "Would you all like caffé?"

"*Non fastidio, non fastidio*" (Don't bother), says Domenica, but the others agree.

Domenica follows me to the kitchen. I fill the bottom of the caffettiera with water and set it on the counter. Immediately Domenica picks it up, checks the water level, and decides to add a little more. I put the fine, powdered caffé into the basket and proceed to set it into the water when Domenica reaches for the metal container, takes it from my hand, clucks her tongue, shakes her head at me, and spoons in a little more caffé. While she is preparing the tray with china, I unwrap a package of chocolate and vanilla biscotti.

"Oh, *molto cara, molto cara, Adriana.*" (Too expensive.)   This is said with a triple cluck and more head shaking.

"Nonsense, *andiamo a tavola*" (let's go to the table), I respond, as I've had enough of Domenica's cautions.

There is a knock at the door. "Excuse me." I blot my mouth, laying the napkin on the table and answer the door. Totó enters with a very serious expression. His head is low. "Is something wrong?" I inquire.

"Sì, sì, é terribile, é terribile." He walks into the dining room.

Sofia looks up with a smile on her face, but the expression fades quickly when she sees him. "Toe, *che cosa é successo*?" (What's happened?)

"Barbara, she's dead."

Sofia grabs her throat, and the others gasp.

"*Quando*?" Tiziana asks.

"*Stamattina.*" (This morning.)

I can follow the conversation to this point, but now everyone starts talking at once and I am lost.   Sofia's heavy breathing and intermittent deep groaning begins to resemble a large bellows.   Our attention is drawn to her as she raises her large frame from the table.   I begin to wonder if we are witnessing a metamorphosis as she begins walking around the spacious room bellowing, ranting and raving.   When we think she has run down, she mumbles, gestures, and revs up again.

"Totó, is Sofia alright?"

"Ya, ya, ya, Sofia loves to get herself worked up, like. Don't give any notice to her."

"Who is Barbara? How did she die?"

"She is that pretty little dark-haired girl up the street. Her daddy took her out for walks."

"Oh, I know who you are talking about. Sometimes they walked the same way Bridgie and I do."

"Well, Signora, it's like this. She got the flu the other day and they put her in the hospital. The doctor said she was better

62

and could go home. So, they brought her home last evening, and she died this morning."

"That's terrible!"

"Yes. Her father said he's goin' to have that bloody, no good doctor taken care of -- if you know what I mean!"

I shake my head soberly. The whole thing is so barbaric. Imagine a child dying of the flu in 1988.

*

That evening Gaines and I sit in the living room after Bridget's nightly inspection, waiting for dinner to cook.

"What happened today?"

"I'm mystified, baffled, bewildered, perplexed and downright confused," Gaines declares, shaking his head.

"What?" My curiosity is peaked.

"Well, it's as if they went around the office and found the least qualified person they could possibly find. When they made her discovery, they said, 'Congratulations, you have been rewarded for your simple-mindedness, you get to be the secretary to the Director of Engineering.' "

I sit with a smile on my face, amused at Gaines' rendition. He continues, "She can't type worth a darn. Can't take dictation. Can't speak or understand English. Can't get herself to the office half the time. Can't do anything that I tell her to do, and she can't keep her mouth shut while I struggle with Italian trying to tell her something. In all my twenty-eight years of working, I've never seen anyone that can equal her incompetence."

"What does she do when she is there?"

Gaines lowers his head in reflection, twisting the hair of his sideburn between his thumb and index finger. He starts laughing, shaking his head. "She stands at the coffee machine and sings Sinatra's song, 'Strangers in the Night.' " Gaines imitates her singing with an Italian accent.

Fruttivendolo.

10

The postman's bell is immediately followed by the clop-clop sound of wooden sandals making contact with the hard surface of the cortile. From the dining room which provides a lovely view of the cortile and front gate, I observe Totó's race to get the mail. He stoops to gather the scattered envelopes that don't manage to stay secure on the back of the scooter, scrutinizing both the front and back of each piece, he sorts the mail and climbs the steps, stretching on his tiptoes, he stands the envelopes in the windowsill next to our front door.

This little scene is played out every day. Finally, the mailbox from Fernanda is delivered. With it comes the hope of some privacy. Sofia looks out and sees me and Bridget coming down the stairs and opens the door. "You all right?"

"Sì. And you?"

"Fine, thanks. Come on in." Sofia motions with her arm never taking her eyes from the box.

Totó is perched on the little day bed pulling socks over his bare feet and puffing frantically in order to cloud his lungs with the required drug, not troubling himself to remove the noxious weed, he says, "Here comes trouble!" to Bridgie as she walks past him on her way to the kitchen for goodies. "Buon giorno, Signora. What's ya got there?"

I hold out the box and cautiously say, "Well, this was given to us, and we thought it would be handy for all of us to use."

Sofia displays ready enthusiasm as Totó feigns indifference. Hoping he doesn't suspect the box is from Fernanda, I quietly await his reaction. "Just put it there like," pointing to the coffee table. "I'll see what can be done with the bloody nuisance." He has it mounted in fifteen minutes and hurries to the gate when he hears il postino's bell up the street. Totó proudly informs him where the new box is located. Old ways are difficult to forsake and just like Pavlov's dog, the familiar scene repeats itself. When il postino sounds his bell, Totó hastens to the box, sorts the mail with careful inspection of each piece and places our letters on the sill. I realize that we will always be under the watchful eye of "The One Who Has To Know All."

Monday through Saturday the cacophonous buzzing of three-wheeled trucks, *ape* (wasp), can be heard throughout Lecce. They are laden with fresh fruits and vegetables and several of these insect mimesis harshly whir up Via dei Sepolcri Messapici routinely. I hear one coming and hurry to get my shopping basket and some money. The *fruttivendolo* (fruit and vegetable vendor), stands in the street shouting his produce. One little weasel-like housewife scurries out of her slot in the wall and approaches the truck She instantly puts her hand to her mouth, bites the side of it, and scampers back to her abode. I observe this peculiar little performance, but put the thought aside and go about buying the locally grown vegetables.

I am met with friendly prying as I enter the gate. "Going to cook today?"

"Yes, and I would appreciate either you or Sofia giving me some information regarding seasoning for these particular greens. I look at Totó and bite my hand as the neighbor had done at the fruttivendolo's ape. "Totó, what does this mean?"

"It means, I forgot. You've got a lot to learn about us and our ways."

"Oh! Don't remind me!"

Later, I open the door to that loud familiar knock. Totó steps past me and starts down the hallway toward the kitchen, barking orders with all of the impertinence of a chief surgeon about to perform a quadruple bypass on my kitchen table. "Now, get out a sharp paring knife and a large pot with a lid.

And you'll need a colander. This here is *barbabietole* (green tops of beets). Wash it good, like under running water."

His instructions are solicitously obeyed and we watch the reddish soil disappear down the drain. A snail shell is flushed out of one of the leaves. Totó picks it up and as he pitches it in the garbage bag says, "*Lumàca*, this is good too!" He fills the pot with water and adds vegetable bouillon cubes. When it starts to boil, he immerses the leaves. "Now, cook until tender. It only takes a few minutes, like. Serve with grated *parmigiano-reggiano* and fresh bread. *Una rosetta* is best, it's a roll or bun with a flower design on it." He puts his finger in the center of his cheek and says, "É buono." On the marble countertop he sees a baking dish full of a yellow mixture which is the consistency of bread pudding or dressing. He almost recoils, points to it, and asks with a display of squeamishness, "What's that?"

"It's polenta, Totó. Don't you care for it ?"

Dismally he curls his lip and adds with a grimace, "Oh, it's all right for thems that likes it!"

Chuckling at his remark, "Good grief, Totó! You who eat eel, snails, tripe, and nerves the Lord only knows what that is. Not to mention flavoring your sugo with the juice of 'old Dobbin,' turn your nose up at unpolluted grain innocent cornmeal flavored with sauteed onions, red pepper, butter, and salt. I can't believe it. Mamma mia!" I exclaim throwing my hands in the air.

My minuscule harangue amuses him. "You'll get along just fine here, Signora. Now I have to go down and see about me own dinner."

"Totó," I reach into the *frigorifero* (refrigerator) and hand him another vegetable.

"What is this and how is it prepared?"

"This here is *finocchio*," he takes it and loosens the stalks and rinses them under running water and cuts a piece. "Here taste it."

"It tastes like licorice, it is fennel."

"You eat it fresh, like, after a large meal. It is a *digestivo*, it helps the digestion. Some people bake it with cheese but I prefer it fresh, like. *Multi anni fa* (many years ago), queers was boiled in water with finocchio, that's why they are called *finocchii* today."

"You are a wealth of information today, Totó."

"Send *Briginella* (Bridgie) down after awhile."

I shake my head as he walks out of sight, looking at the redhead lying on the kitchen floor, "Now your name has been changed to Briginella!"

11

Gaines enters il nido, pours his first cup of coffee from the Bunn-o-Matic, and takes plastic wrap off the cereal bowl that was placed on the butler's tray last night. Ice cream is the only dairy product that this Iowa farm boy ever allows to enter his mouth, so the traditional milk or cream is omitted from his bran flakes. I converted to his way because it serves in eliminating a few more daily calories.

Most of our early mornings are spent in silence nursing the caffeine in order to awaken ourselves from a zombielike state as neither one of us are morning people. We refer to this early morning condition as being open or closed. Between gulps of hot brew that washes down the chewy bland fodder, we watch in silence the morning news program, which is an Italian version of the Today Show.

Gaines picks scattered pieces of the fly-away grains from his napkin and initiates some chitchat. "Are you open yet?"

I swallow the last drop of my first cup. "I suppose. Are you?"

"Would you be interested in helping an Italian girl with English?"

"Come again."

"Her father works at the plant. Yesterday he came into my office and asked if you would be interested in helping his daughter with English?"

"He doesn't even know me!" I shake my head with puzzlement. "Well, yes. I guess I could help her. I certainly need more to do. Tell him yes. Gaines, have you heard any more about the telephone? It has been almost a month since you

69

paid the deposit. Fernanda had a phone in the short space of time she lived here. The house is already wired, so what is it?"

"I'm as angry as you are. All I get at the office is, 'Oh, you live in the old city. It is very difficult in that part of town.' One of my Italian colleagues suggested finding a neighbor to share a line with."

"Well, I'll ask Totó. Maybe the Signorina or Domenica has one. I'll check with Domenica this evening when she comes to oversee the Caffé making. I didn't tell you what she did yesterday."

"What?"

"She came in, began turning off some of the lights, clucked her tongue, and said *"Conservo, Adriana, conservo!"* She also checked the thermostat to see what I had it set on. Totó is right she is a 'bloody nuisance.' "

"Well, their attitude towards us is that we can't do anything until it comes time to pay for something, then we are accepted as their equals." He smiles at the thought of Domenica going around turning out the lights and checking the thermostat.

"Our class with George Whitecotton starts tonight. No one is very excited about going to him for Italian classes. I can't quite put my finger on it but there is something kinky about him."

"Why is an Englishman our Italian teacher anyway? Wouldn't it be better to learn from a native Leccese? I really don't understand their thinking at the company."

"Ha, ha, ha! *Chi sa*?" (Who knows?) Oh! surely he has an under-the-table deal with Riso, *lui é molto importante!*" (He is very important!)

"I'll be ready about quarter to six." Bridget and I walk Gaines to the front door, say our goodbyes, and go to the French doors in the guest room. I pull them open and lean on the decorative rail. We watch him leave the gate underneath and follow him through the narrow stone passageway swinging his briefcase. He turns to wave before leaving.

"Are you ready to go shopping Briginella, or do you want to stay in the cortile?"

70

I juggle the metal shopping cart down the stairs, and Bridget assists by placing her jaws over my instep and holding it with her mouth until my foot is moved to the next step. She repeats the action on the opposite foot. "Bridget, one of these days your herding instinct is going to make me fall!"

Reaching the cortile, I collapse the cart and start toward the gate when Sophia appears from the two-room compartment under the stairs. She is carrying yesterday's just-laundered intimate wear and places the pieces on the drying rack in the view of all who pass number twenty-four Sepolcri Messapici.

"You all right?"

"Yes! Thanks, Sofia. And you?"

"Oh, *Non c'é male*." (Not bad.)

Totó comes out from under the stairs, clutching white powder in his fists. He stoops over each potted plant and works the fine powder into the soil with his hands. "We don't use them bloody contraptions around here," he says, motioning toward the cart.

"How inconvenient for you. Totó, how long did it take for you all to get a telephone when you moved from England?"

"Oh, it was already here. Me mother, she had one. But I had SIP, that's the telephone company, come and take the bloody nuisance out, like."

"Why did you do that?"

"Oh! Sofia called everybody she ever knew in England, and the bloody bill was so high I couldn't stand it so I had it removed."

"Wouldn't it have been simpler to tell her not to call everyone she ever knew in England?"

When Totó isn't smoking or eating, he is usually whistling or singing. He is happy caring for plants and cooking. He grows everything in terra cotta pots - herbs, plants, and flowers. There is a recessed place, an absence of a stone in the wall below the outside stairway. This morning he decides to put a small pot of beautiful, pink, vined geraniums in that empty space, so he

Geraniums and Bridget's water pan.

hammers thin nails in the mortar to hold up the blossom-laden branches.

In two hours I return from shopping and stop to admire his handiwork. He comes from the area under the stairs with an oil can and stoops to lubricate the wheels on the "bloody contraption." He then lifts my morning's purchases from the cart and sets them on the bottom step.

"Now, you can just keep this thing in here, like." He picks it up, puts it in the first room under the stairs, and returns carrying a new, turquoise plastic pan which is full of water. He carefully sets it down next to the wall across from the doorway leading into the compartment. Bridget runs and laps up some of the cool, fresh water. Totó looks at me with an impish grin.

Sofia, moving a little faster these days, bounds out of the house wiping her hands on her apron, calls "Toe," goes into the chattering of the unknown tongue and then disappears under the stairs. He looks at me with amusement and waits for Sofia's return. She brings out an old, weathered box made from wooden slats and sets the shallow water pan on top of it. Bridget tries it out, and sure enough, the dog will never again have to lower her pretty head for a drink in the cortile.

We all laugh. "You're spoiling her!" I exclaim. Bridget is very good for Sofia. She'll help her get over Randy. Sofia talks to her all the time, and it seems that Briginella is the only one outside of Totó and Stefania who really understands Sofiaese. Their house has become the dog's second home.

Briginella doesn't stand on ceremony, such as waiting to be invited inside. She's intuitive enough to perceive their attitude toward her and lets herself inside their home by giving the French door a hearty slap of the paw, which creates a design of linear grooves on the outside facing. Most people consider it unsightly, but the *Famiglia di* Totó always welcome her lovingly. Stefania says, "Briginella, ciao bella mia." Sofia utters a phrase that only Bridgie and God understand. Totó's greeting is affectionate and dramatically expressed, "Here comes <u>Trouble</u>!"

Bridget sashays through the front room, Stefania's bedroom, and back to the tiny kitchen in the rear. She takes her post under a small, square-shaped table, anticipating tasty morsels of pasta *al forno, parmigiana di melanzane, spaghetti al sugo* and other appetizing delectables created in the poorly arranged and inconvenient cubbyhole known as the kitchen.

It is getting close to noon and I am overcome by the scent of the sauce wafting its way inside my nostrils, causing water to well up in my mouth. As I pass their door, I can't help but think that if a person is a cook, they can practice the art anywhere.

"Let me help you with them packages," Totó says, as he gathers up the plastic bags he had placed on the steps a few minutes ago. He motions for me to go ahead of him and sets the parcels on the kitchen table, reviewing what has been bought that morning by carefully observing the contents of the open bags.

Nothing escapes him, I think. His twisted little brain is making calculations so fast he's apt to have a meltdown right here in my <u>chicken</u>! He notices the purchase of mozzarella *di bufola*, gesturing with a cock of his head, "That's a bloody expensive type of mozzarella to be buying. It's very dear, very dear indeed!"

Feeling it is none of his business, I try to ignore his prying nature but am disturbed by his relentless interference in our business as well as his voicing critical assumptions and making meddlesome calculations. I attempt to redirect his attention, feeling an intrusive reproof coming, so I decide on a tactic of distraction. "Totó, when I hear Sofia speak to you and Stefania, it sort of sounds like Italian, but I can't understand a thing she says. Is it the dialect of her home region?"

Totó looks at me in all seriousness and says. "Oh, don't bother trying to understand what Sofia babbles. No one understands her. The fact of the matter is, Sofia doesn't speak any language!" With that pronouncement he leaves. "Send the *Principessa* down after while and I'll take her out." He barks from the corridor and slams the door. I shake my head and laugh out loud, reflecting on his droll explanation of Sofia's language traits.

*

This evening as we leave for class, Gaines and I are bundled up as if we're in a midwestern snowstorm. We are trying to ward off the penetrating winds from mother Russia that were forecast for today and tomorrow. "Do you want to go the front way or the back?"

"The shortest way," I answer, shivering.

"They are about the same. Let's take the back way this evening to avoid the traffic."

Walking on the back side of St. Irene's Church and School is somewhat like passing into another realm for a few minutes. It is dimly lit, not ghostly quiet, but neither is it eerie. The hulking sidewalls tower above miniaturizing any object in juxtaposition. Sometimes the pipes of the antique organ are heard bellowing out into the stone gallery, legitimizing the ecclesiastical backdrop and embellishing the periodic figures emerging in dark habits. They sweep the gritty stone on their little missions of scholastic or deiform nature through the walkway.

"This is my favorite way to walk to the Piazza, Gaines. It seems so serene and mysterious. Almost reeks of hallowed ground. Do you feel it?"

"Well, to me it reeks of purse snatchers and muggers!" Gaines says, as he grips my wool-sheathed hand and quickens our pace to the well-lighted front entrance of St. Irene, where the two courses converge. We leave solemnitude for the liveliness and motion of the Leccese night life which is in full swing. The variety of one-owner shops are sockets of brightly colored jewels on both sides of the street, like two strands of lights laid out to the Piazza.

We meet Bobby, Margie, Chet, Norma, and Tom on the crowded thoroughfare, scrunched in coupling or triplet fashion and chatting as we forge ahead to class. We resort to single file when space denies our togetherness because of the narrowing

75

sidewalk or when facing a group of natives knotted together, disallowing us elbowroom, requiring us to relinquish our space.

The Italian attitude must be learned by us seven newcomers, because we have been steeped in putting the other person first. That simply is not done in the streets of Italy, and if a person is naive enough to try and practice it, they will either be looked on as a fool or simply *pazzo* (crazy). This goes for driving as well as walking, and in some bizarre sense it gives one a feeling of belonging when we finally arrive and cut the other person out of his space or turn. There is a method to their system of madness, and amazingly enough one encounters *pochi incidenti* (few accidents.)

Still inside of the historic district, we leave the lighted Piazza and turn onto a narrow alleyway leading to the Whitecotton Language Studio. The school as well as George and Elsa's living quarters take up the entire second floor of the seventeenth century palazzo. It can be seen at the end where the alley turns left and becomes a dead end.

When we arrive at the corner, two lighted ground floor apartments reveal gaudily dressed women advertising from the tawdry front rooms. We turn from the grotesque sight and hasten to the huge portal facing us.

Pushing the buzzer, we wait in the frigid air for the sound of the lock release. Walking through the porte-co-chere, we are compelled to step over the restorer's tools which are strewn about as if they had been dropped in place at "quittin' time" around a portable cement mixer which has been left in the path of traffic. We take the triple marble staircase with a massive balustrade. The grit and cement particles travel with us, embedding themselves into the soles of our shoes.

The smell of oil from a heater greets us as we enter the classroom. This greeting is more than any from our instructor, who is seated at the table writing. We had met Whitecotton on a pervious visit to Italy, but he doesn't notice us. We sit around three long tables which form a U shape facing the rotund, short man with a ruddy complexion who's bearing a striking resemblance to a very well-known English actor.

"Have any of you Americans ever studied a foreign language before?" He looks at each of us going around the room we nod "no" except for me and Bobby. "When we were small, we were at war in Europe and the Pacific. It's not like it is here with other countries bordering so close, making it easy and necessary to learn other languages. Until the late fifties people didn't do a lot of foreign traveling either. Languages just weren't encouraged when we were in school as they are now especially in the Midwest," explains Gaines.

"Yes, I've heard it's rather backward." Whitecotton responds.

"Well, don't believe everything you hear!" shoots Margie. Everyone smiles, including the professor, who decides she can pay for her little retort.

"Okay, Signora Robson, why don't you go through the first exercise for us."

Whitecotton remains aloof throughout the class period until he hands out printed lists of the irregular verbs as an assignment for the next class period. "Now, have you made plans for dinner this evening?"

"Nowhere in particular," Chet answers, "Just a *Trattoria* (cafe) nearby."

"Could I make a suggestion?" He offers while smiling and becoming friendly.

"Sure," Margie answers.

"There is a good place that I frequent nearby. One can take their buffet or order from a menu. However, I'll have to walk you there because these winding, narrow streets are a little tricky to the foreigners. I think you'll like it; the food is Leccese specialties and it is inexpensive."

Norma and I exchange a glance and the same thought: Whitecotton has just finagled his way into our dinner party.

La Capannina (The Little Hut) is close and has an appealing atmosphere. An attractive waiter in a white jacket and black trousers leads us into a room where the eight of us are seated comfortably at three white-clothed, square tables placed together.

"Bring a bottle of Salice Salentino," George tells the waiter in Italian.

He returns with a corkscrew, white cloth, and dusty bottle. With a certain flair he displays his expertise of opening the wine, pours a taste for George, and waits for his remarks. The Englishman relishes the attention and shares his knowledge of the fruit of the vine, which seems somewhat pretentious to us Midwesterners.

Norma, seated next to me, leans near and whispers, "He loves an audience!"

"Sì, sì." I agree.

George plays the host of the party and fills the glasses, emptying the contents of the bottle. Catching the waiter's eye, George motions him to bring another bottle of the same.

Chet proposes a toast. "If we were all there, we wouldn't be here." We repeat it and Gaines says, "Here, here." "*Saluti*," we say as we touch glasses and eat *grissini*, thin breadsticks from Torino.

Before the order is placed, Whitecotton has downed three-quarters of the second bottle, empties the remainder into Chet's, Bobby's, and Tom's glasses and orders a third bottle. With each passing swallow, his behavior becomes more aggressive, mean-spirited, and contemptible. He points his finger at me across the table and says, "I'm going to be so hard on you in this class," laughing loudly. I ignore his prediction, assuming it is *troppo vino* talking.

At the end of the second plate (meat and vegetable), four bottles of Salice Salentino have been finished off by Whitecotton, and he is promoting San Marzano (herbal liqueur, speciality of Puglia) for an after-dinner drink.

George has conveniently left his wallet and credit cards behind and is suggesting a stop at the Risorgimento Hotel for a nightcap. Everyone has to get home and hightails it, thus leaving Whitecotton to enter the hotel by himself.

Gaines and I take the busy, lighted side of St. Irene's back to the house and see Totó's arms hanging through the spaces of the vertical rungs. His foot rests on the base of the partially opened gate.

"There he is behind bars probably where he belongs," I say softly, as we near the entrance.

While holding the rungs, he steps backward, making room for us to enter the cortile. "I just took her out." Looking up, Totó motions with his thumb. "She done her business and a bit of a wee."

"Thanks, Totó." I smile at him.

His head tilted back, he looks up at Gaines and removes his cigarette as we walk toward the stairs.

"I've got this nephew, you see. My sister's boy. He needs a job, like."

Gaines is getting his drift. "What does he do?"

Totó chuckles. "Not a bloody thing. That's why he needs a job!"

Gaines cuts through his nonsense to inquire, "Does he have training for anything?"

"Oh, they calls it *Geometra* or something like that."

"Totó, I don't do any hiring at the plant. That is a job for personnel."

"Ya, ya, but you could suggest him, like."

Gaines does not want to get involved and changes the subject. "Who of the neighbors around here has a phone?"

Totó removes the ash-laden prop from his lips and flips the particles to the courtyard. Disinterestedly he cocks his head to the right, "Oh, there's this one here and then there's that other one over there." He nods to the left, conveying his dislike for the last one mentioned.

"Okay, Totó! Thanks for helping with Bridget. Buona notte."

"*Non fa niente.* (It is nothing.) Buona notte."

I hang up my coat in the guest room closet, walk to the French doors and start to close the wooden inside shutters, when I notice a neighbor, Signore Albanese, standing in the street looking up to his son's French doors. Franco, his son, lives next door above Domenica.

"Gaines, come here, isn't that sweet. Every night he goes out for a walk and comes by to tell his son goodnight below the balcony."

"Yes, I've seen him come by before, when I've taken Bridgie out."

I turn on the dishwasher as I pass the kitchen and put a bottle of water on the breakfast tray which I had prepared earlier.

"What did you think of class this evening?" Gaines asks as he takes his pajamas from the chest of drawers.

"I feel disappointed and let down by the company for hiring someone like Whitecotton. His name should be cottonmouth, after the snake I believe he is. One of my goals in coming over here is to learn the language. He isn't the least bit interested in teaching us Italian."

"Well, we're not going to be manipulated into going to dinner with him again. I'm not going to buy his dinner and booze, and then have to listen to his drunken talk. We'll just make other arrangements."

"Bridgie, are you going to join us?" The dog jumps on the bed, twirls around spinning herself close to an orbit state, and flops herself next to my rib cage. "Oh, Bridget! Someday you're going to knock the wind out of me. You vixen!" The dog nestles into the curve of my body on top of the covers and the three of us snuggle together as drowsiness edges out all that matters.

The ear-piercing sound of the buzzer bores into our slumber, jolting our tranquility. Bridget leaps off the bed, barking all the way down the stairs, hoists her front legs to the glass panels in the French doors, and threatens the encroachment at the security gate. Gaines and I follow her, putting on robes, and trying to work our bare feet into slip-ons.

"Oh, good grief! It's Domenica. What in the world does she want?" Gaines fumbles with the door latch. "Bridget, shut up! It's only Domenica." We step out onto the balcony.

"Hush up! You're going to wake everyone in the neighborhood!" I try to calm Bridgie down.

Gaines grabs the agitated pet by the collar, pushing her inside, and pulls the door closed so we can hear what our neighbor is saying.

Domenica is yelling, "*Acqua, acqua.*" Pointing to the outside stairs. She is pulling her hair and waving her arms. "Oh, *Madonna! Acqua. acqua.*"

We can see the water pouring out from under our front door creating a splendid waterfall splashing down the stone stairs. We dash into the kitchen. Gaines turns off the dishwasher, scoots it from under the counter. "One of the hoses has come off." He secures it, and we mop up the water. I turn the machine on again and immediately the electrifying buzzer is heard once more. This sends Bridget back to deafening barks. She beats us onto the balcony and Gaines takes her by the collar and shoves her inside again.

"*Cosa sta succedendo?*" (What is happening?) Domenica asks. "*Posso aiutarvi?*" (Can I help you all?)

"No, grazie, Domenica. Va tutto bene. *La lavastoviglie sta perdendo acqua.*" (The dishwasher is leaking water.)

She smiles and waves to us. "Buona notte."

"Buona notte, Domenica." We wave back and enter the house.

Domenica returns to her small, ground floor apartment next door. Tiziana is still up so Domenica is able to share the little drama with her daughter.

"Oh, their friends at San Cataldo, I'll call them! They should be told."

"Mamma, no. You'll only wake them up. Besides everything is okay now." Tiziana pleads to no avail.

Domenica finds their number and dials. "Oh, mamma mia." Tiziana throws up her hands and leaves the room.

81

Out at the beach, Chet and Margie are awakened by the phone from a sound sleep. He looks at the clock. It is 11:45 p.m. "The call must be from the States."

"I hope everything is okay," Margie says, as she sits up in bed and listens to his end of the conversation.

"Oh, sì, Domenica. *Come va?* Now, *piano, piano. Io non capisco bene.* (Speak slowly. I don't understand well.)

"You mean to tell me that Domenica called out here to tell us that the Grant's dishwasher overflowed and that's it? Well, what did she think we could do about it? Wake us up out of a sound sleep! Oh, Eyetalians! I don't understand the way they think. Nor do I understand why the company hired an Englishman to teach us Eyetalian! He's a mess!" Margie utters as she rolls over on her stomach, socks her feather pillow, and says, "Good night, Darlin'!"

*

The next morning as Gaines drives to work he longs for the green fields of corn and soybeans, for a disciplined and organized people with principles of morality, character, and integrity with whom to live and work. However, he is determined not to back out of his contract and will stay to the end of it, knowing he can count on me and together we will make the best of a difficult situation. That is how we have lived our twenty-eight years of marriage.

It takes fifteen minutes to get to the plant. He drives into a fenced-in area where a uniformed employee from security takes his car and makes notes as to any repairs needed. He asks Gaines if he wants it washed today. Gaines goes to his office, which is on the Adriatic side, and on a clear day he can see the mountains of Albania only fifty miles away.

A knock at the door is followed by his secretary, Signorina Manzoni, announcing Engineer Robson.

"*Per favore, ci porti due caffè*" (Please, bring two coffees), Gaines asks his secretary.

Chet sits down and proceeds to take out his leather pouch and seasoned pipe. He fills the pipe and taps the tobacco in place and starts the lighting process. After his first inhalation, a most satisfying expression is evident and he sits back, stretching out his legs and says, "We got a call last night at a quarter to twelve. Woke us both up. Thought it was Mom or one of the kids, but it was your next door neighbor, Domenica, calling to tell us that your dishwasher overflowed." He starts to chuckle. "I don't know what she thought we could do about it out at San Cataldo."

Gaines starts to smile and shakes his head. "I don't know why she called you. We didn't ask her."

Gaines becomes agitated about several things. "Isn't that just like them? They act on impulse without ever giving thought to the other person. Do you know that over a month ago I paid a deposit of $180 to the phone company. Haven't seen a telephone yet, nor do we have a promise of one. None of us can have a bank account because they are so screwed up that they can't get our work visas. And another thing, Bobby came in here the other day wanting to know when we were going to get paid. I asked him if he needed money. He said he didn't and that he was okay. But after all it has been over a month, and we haven't seen anything yet. Oh, I tried to talk to that Riso about it. He said that we could take a cash advance from the cashier if we needed money. He's worthless, absolutely worthless! I'll tell you, Chet, this is the most unprofessional mess I've ever seen. Another thing, that Giovanni out there on the board, next to Bobby, this just blows my mind. He used to be in the Carabiniere Police. Well, he had a pretty bad accident on the job, which left him mentally impaired for gosh sakes. So what do they do with him? Give him a job in engineering. The absurdity of it all is mind boggling. And to top it off, Riso has hired that overbearing Whitecotton to be our Italian teacher of all things. They must have a deal!"

Gaines and Chet start laughing and simultaneously say, "If we were all there, we wouldn't be here!"

Signorina Manzoni brings in the caffè.

"Grazie, Signorina." Gaines commences to give her instructions, when she rudely interrupts him. His face becomes flushed, he stands and points at her. *"Aspetti."* (You wait.) He finishes with his instructions, and then she leaves the office frowning. "That's another thing. I've got to get a real secretary."

12

The sun is pouring into il nido this morning. Its rays hamper Gaines' vision on the right side. He is seated on the sofa having his first cup of coffee and watching Maria Grazia present the latest news on television.

I come in, take the plastic wrap from my dry cereal, and pour a cup of coffee. "Are you ready for another?"

He holds out the cup and saucer. "Thanks."

Bridget positions herself on the sofa next to Gaines in the sun splotch and basks in its warmth.

"Daniela D'Amelio will be brought here about four o'clock this afternoon by her mother."

"Fine," I say, handing him his cereal.

"Luigi, her father, said he would be by for her about five-thirty or whenever he can get away from work."

"Did you find out how much English she has had?"

"Luigi said she is in her third year."

About five minutes before four o'clock, Bridget and I go into the guest room and look onto the street, which has not yet come to life. A motorcar can be heard in the distance, and as the sound heightens, the object materializes and skirts the furniture shop in a rollicking manner. The *Cinquecento* is a miniature motorcar which has not been in production for sixteen years. There are many running the roads, streets, and thoroughfares of Italy. They are highly coveted not only by the natives, but by foreigners as well. The itsy-bitsy car advances with all the speed it can muster on the somewhat choppy stone surface. It is lurching, swerving, and veering toward the gate below. I watch the charge aimed at the house and fear the driver isn't going to manage the necessary stop. But the time-worn vehicle proves to

85

be functional, acquiescing to its driver's demands. Mother and daughter abandon the automobile, slamming the doors as they exit.

Giuliana and her daughter, Daniela, enter the previously unlocked security gate. La mamma is aware of all that surrounds them as they proceed through the foliage-laden cortile. She remarks on this and that, displaying knowledge of the plant life that surrounds them as well as enthusiasm for its existence. I am waiting outside the front door on the landing and extend my hand to Giuliana, who leads the ascent. She seizes my hand and pulls me to her, enabling her to give me the cheek-to-cheek greeting. She does the talking in lickety-split Italian and orchestrates her daughter behind her into position so she, too, can mimic her mother's greeting whether Daniela wants to or not! She is pretty, tall, softly spoken, and shy. Daniela obviously takes a back seat to her vivacious, beautiful little mama as everyone else probably does.

Giuliana's departure is as boisterous and vocal as her entrance but is completed momentarily. This woman doesn't let any grass grow under her feet! As Giuliana slams the gate, Daniela exhales with a sigh of relief. She smiles at me and says, "Oh, mamma, youa willa ava tua geta usea tua era."

I return the smile knowing exactly where to begin with Daniela's English. "Would you like a Nutella snack?"

"Si, oh yes. Thanks!"

"Actually, Daniela, your English is quite good. Why don't we take our snack into the living room and get acquainted. You need to drop the vowel at the end of the word. As we visit keep that in mind." She has brought her English Literature book, and I help her with vocabulary as well as comprehension.

The lesson time goes fast and her father arrives at the appointed time. He has a good build, handsome face, and he is prematurely bald. He, like his wife, doesn't speak English, but his Italian is much slower and easier to follow. Daniela does the translating during our brief visit, and as I walk them to the door,

86

he turns and tells me something in Italian. I look to Daniela for interpretation.

"My father says thata you will ava your telephone ina five days."

"What?"

"My father saida, thata you will ava your telephone in five days." She shrugs at me, as if to let me know that she, herself, doesn't know anything about it.

"Thank you. Oh, scusi, grazie molto, Signor D'Amelio, grazie."

"*Di niente.* (It is nothing.) Buona sera, Signora."

"Buona sera, Signor, buona sera, Daniela."

"Calla me Dani. Everyone does."

"Goodbye, Dani. See you next Tuesday."

I re-enter the house in contemplation. If I hadn't agreed to help his daughter with her English, no telling when we'd get a phone if ever! The next time I hear some spoiled American complain about Bell or AT&T, I swear that I'll kick them in the shins!

*

True to Luigi D'Amelio's word, it is five days later and our phone is installed. The line is shared with Domenica. She is most agreeable to giving up her private line status because a duplex is less expensive. Maybe this was a factor as well, but who would ever know for sure. Anyway, I am happy to give Dani an hour and a half each week in exchange for a phone hookup. One hand washes the other, as they say.

As soon as riposo is over, the caffé foursome parade into my living room to see the little "black beauty" sitting on the chest. Domenica, Tiziana, Sofia and Stefania express their happiness for us. Each one says "*Auguri*" (Best wishes) and gives me a cheek to cheek!

"Gaines, I can't believe the whole thing. From the way we got the phone to the neighbors' reaction. I feel like we ought to name it and send out announcements! One would think the neighbors were coming to admire a new baby. It's unbelievable."

Stretching the absurdity, he says, "We could have a christening at the Duomo and give all the guests *Bomboniere* (special gifts given to guests who attend christenings, confirmations and weddings) too!"

13

Each Friday morning is commemorated with the familiar acknowledgment of T.G.I.F., thank God it's Friday. It has special significance to us because we have survived another week of this fatiguing lifestyle.

Gaines finds apartment living in the historic quarter to be quite confining. He is homesick this morning. A place that grows rocks in red soil among the olive orchards, vineyards, and artichoke fields is a little too exotic for his tastes. He yearns for the sight of rolling hills, forests, and fields and almost daily threatens to return to the States and buy a house in the middle of forty acres! We are lethargically sipping the day's first cup of coffee in il nido and only quiet utterances are made by either of our partially opened selves.

Friday is also the day that the house has a thorough going over. Domenica has campaigned for Tiziana to work for us, but with Totó's belittling and discrediting of her and every poor soul that is suggested for the job, he has jockeyed himself into the position of being our weekly cleaner and overseer.

"Are you open?" asks Gaines.

"Almost."

"Try to find out from Totó where I can get heels put on those black wingtips."

"Will do."

One hour later, I set the shoes on the buffet chest in the dining room and speak to Totó, who has let himself in to start the weekly cleaning. His arms are wrapped around an Oriental rug as he takes it out on the balcony to shake and leave on the railing for an airing. Yet to be done is the week's dust, grit, and fine wisps of long red hair that have to be sought out from hidden corners.

"What are you going to do with them shoes?"

"Oh, they need new heels. Can you tell me where the shoe repair is located?"

He takes the cigarette from his lips with thumb and middle finger. Turning his palm upward innovating a receptacle for the fly-away particles and once again practicing his gift of evasiveness gives his noggin' a one-time toss, "Oh, there's that one down there."

I draw a deep breath, purposely close my eyelids trying to calm my impatience with his incessant vagueness. "Would it be asking too much for you to break your vow of secrecy just this once and tell me who you are referring to and where it is that he has a shop, hum?"

"Just leave 'em there, like. I'll take care of it."

"Va bene! I'm going to Norma's new apartment. After she gives me the guided tour, we're going to the big market. It's real close to her house. I want to take the shopping cart. Is the compartment under the stairs unlocked?"

"Sì, Signora. Now, enjoy yourself and don't let them bloody vendors take advantage of you!"

After weeks of searching for an apartment, Tom and Norma have left the Hotel Tiziana. Tom Browning is an engineer not just through education but deep into the marrow of his bones. He approaches everything with a slowly thought-out, analytical study. This man is the S. Holmes of the group, probing all aspects with consideration, contemplation, examination, and thoughtful research.

But unlike the famous investigator, something seems to go awry in Tom's perfectly laid plans. The apartment hunt is a perfect example. As well as scrutinizing the choices of their American colleagues, Tom and Norma have combed every corner of Lecce. Since parking is a pain and the raffish appearance holds no appeal for them, the historic district was eliminated right off. The beach has a calling for Tom, but the isolation is forbidding to Norma.

Finally, modern Lecce is searched out and selected: The lovely apartment is spacious and well-furnished with a gorgeous kitchen. It has a garage under the building, and each renter has a private, locked box for their car and storage space. A security gate surrounds the premises. For added protection a very large, vicious German shepherd lives in the front garden and takes delight in frightening everyone who comes around visitors as well as the tenants. Tom even declares that the apartment is situated so that the afternoon sun does not even shed its rays onto their side of the building, making it far more comfortable since air conditioning is unheard of for most private dwellings.

The walk from my gate to Norma's is rich in layers of the past. I leave narrow passages lined with Baroque architecture, cross the old Piazza surrounded by a Roman Amphitheater second century A.D., the old Town Hall built at the end of the sixteenth century, and annexed to it is a little square church built in 1543 by a colony of Venetian merchants. A Roman column is topped with a fifteen foot bronze statue of the first Bishop of Lecce, Saint Oronzo. The Piazza is named for him. The column is one of a pair that marked the entrance to the Appian way overlooking the sea in Brindisi harbor. I pass the castle, also sixteenth century, and as I head eastward, I leave the beautiful *palozzos* (palaces), and come into modern Lecce with wide streets, and new store fronts under multistoried apartment beehives. I see the street sign Tommaseo and looking at my watch discover that it only took me twenty-five minutes. That's not a bad walk!

My hand is ready to push Norma's apartment bell when a terrorizing bark startles me from behind and causes me to lean against the bell. In my weakened condition, I turn to face this daunting alarm from the inside garden.

"Who is it?" Comes Norma's voice through the little speaker.

"*Sono Io.*" (It is I.)

91

"Okay, Adrianne." I hear the click of the gate and turn to smile at the threatening fangs while he walks confidently next to his iron restriction. I choose the steps instead of the elevator and quickly reach the second story apartment at the top of the stairs.

"Come in. Want a cup of coffee? It's American, of course. Or caffé lungo as the Eyetalians say."

"Sì, sì. It's a miracle I don't have to ask you for a clean pair of panties after the fright I just had downstairs."

"Oh, that's Igor. Isn't he awful? But, I suppose, necessary."

"I can't wait! Show me your apartment. Your cabinetry is beautiful. What a lucky find! Don't you just love it?"

Norma sighs, "Yes, I like it. But we can't get any sleep!"

"You do look tired, Norma. What's wrong?"

"I know I have dark circles this morning. Well, it's those apes. You know the three-wheeled contraptions the fruttivendoli drive. They make so much noise. Well, every morning at four o'clock, except Sunday, the whole street fills up with them. It seems the wholesale produce warehouse is right over there." She points to the large building on another street in the distance. "All the city's vendors have to come that early every morning to buy their produce. The men stand out here in the street visiting, telling jokes, and laughing. I'm so angry. I'd like to throw a grenade out there in the midst of them."

"I'm sorry. But, of course, we didn't know anything about the wholesale market because we live on the opposite side of town. The Italians never told you all? Are you going to stay?"

"We have to! We paid a deposit and signed a lease."

"It's probably like living next to railroad tracks, Norma. Pretty soon you don't hear the new noise."

We walk from the area of modern apartment buildings with enclosed front gardens to a large open field that has not been developed. People drive over the low curbing and park their cars on the red soil crushing all vegetation. To us it feels like going to a fair. "Look how big it is, Norma. We'll never be able to see it all this morning."

"We have three years."

The biweekly market of Lecce is so widespread that it truly is impossible to see it all in one morning's time. It is multifarious, with sweaters, notions, hardware, cheese, salami, leather goods, furs, furniture, lamps, plants, pictures, vegetables, fruits, all types of clothing from infants to adults, cloth from all over the world, and costume jewelry from Africa and the Far East. Norma and I stop at the pottery, which is set out on a parking lot.

"I like those dishes." Norma says, pointing to a set which has a chanticleer motif.

"Oh, Fernanda has those in the apartment. I believe they are characteristic of the region."

The vendors' shouts of "*scegli, scegli*" (you choose) are ear-piercing.

Norma decides on one piece. "I'm going to start a collection."

"Hey, let's go over to the linens." The linen vendor is a big, burly man who looks like a bouncer in a nightclub. He initiates conversation with us.

"*Questo é un grembiule.*" (This is an apron.) Norma and I try to repeat the phrase.

The vendor corrects us time and time again until he is satisfied we can say it correctly. "*Questo é lenzuolo.* (This is a sheet.) His voice possesses a deep, rich, sonorous quality. He makes us repeat it again and again, then he smiles and cautions us about the thieves who regularly work the crowd. He instructs us on the best way to carry one's purse. We are amused because he looks so ridiculous with Norma's purse tucked up under his armpit.

"Adrianne, I remembered to bring a list of sizes. Let me see, if you wear a size six-and-a half shoe, it is size thirty-six or thirty-seven here."

"Oh, nothing is the same any more, Norma. I want some green beans for this weekend. Bobby comes over for dinner on Saturday evenings, and he and Gaines can put a good-sized dent in a kilo of green beans. I cook them with onion, *pancetta affumicata* (Italian smoked bacon), a little vinegar, and red pepper. Sofia is going to teach me to cook them Italian style with spaghetti, sauce, and cheese. My neighbors use only these skinny little green beans with the dark ends. I think they taste the same. Anyway, today I'm going to buy the American type!" We chuckle.

"Adrianne, I'm sure glad you brought the shopping cart." It is so full we are hanging plastic bags around the side of it."

"Where are we going to eat? I'm starving."

"There's a place near Piazza Mazzini called Raffaello's where we can sit outside under a canopy."

We walk to the restaurant. The white, resin chairs look inviting.

"I love white table cloths, don't you?"

"Yes," responds Norma, looking around at the pines, magnolias and smallish lawn. "But I like green grass better. Oh, I miss grass."

"So do I. It's sheer medicinal. I like it here because the evergreens shield us from all the noise and activity of the Piazza."

The waiter, who is impeccably dressed in somewhat formal attire brings each of us a *rustico*, a three-inch diameter of puffed pastry filled with a piece or two of cooked tomato, fresh mozzarella cheese and a little bechamel sauce.

After lunch we part company. Norma to her modern Lecce and me to centro storico.

Arriving home, I meet Totó coming out of the gate. After an exchange of cordial greetings, I inquire about Gaines' shoes since he wants to wear them to Torino.

"Oh, they'll be ready next week sometime," he says, passing it off nonchalantly.

"Ready, where?"

"Down at the place where I took 'em."

"Totó, if you died, I wouldn't have any idea of where to reclaim his shoes."

He grins mischievously and nods toward Mario's Salumeria. "Ya goes up there, like, and turn right. Down the street on the other side of the bicycle shop."

"Grazie molto, now was that so difficult?"

"I took Briginella out a while ago and she done a bit of a wee. Can ya get channel seven on your tele?"

"I don't know. Why do you ask?"

"Oh, just wondering," he giggles. "Me sister's boy is comin' this evening to meet Gaines."

"Oh, really?" I ask, knowing very well that Gaines has not agreed to help Totó's nephew with employment at the plant.

It has all been orchestrated and clearly thought out by Totó. He informs Sofia that they will play *Scopa* (card game) in the cortile instead of the front room this evening. After riposo the gathering takes place for caffé, cards and *chiacchiera* (gossip). The group is referred to as the covey by the us. The sounds of the shrill, screechy, local dialect resemble a pack of chirpy little game birds.

The regular attenders are Domenica, Tizianna, the septuagenarians Antonia (who is referred to as the Signorina) and her sister, Gabriella, and their upstairs neighbor, Lucia, Stefania, Sofia, and of course, his headship Totó. The firm foam rubber cushions are taken from Sofia's bamboo furniture and are used as substitute tables for the card games. They are supported on the players thighs.

Totó's nephew, Claudio, arrives at six forty-five as prearranged by good ol' Uncle Totó. He is good-looking and Stefania has a crush on him. He sits among the assemblage joking with the Signorina, who bears an uncanny likeness to a gazing gargoyle.

The Signorina and Totó are archrivals and have many combative moments over cards. When she wins, she gloats unceasingly to annoy him. He then tells her the reason she is still a Signorina is that no man could ever stand her because she is so

95

bloody mean whereupon she throws her head back and peels with laughter.

Totó has arranged tonight's introduction between Claudio and Gaines to improve Totó's standing among his siblings because he has an ongoing feud with one of his brothers. He hasn't spoken to him for months. If Totó can help find good, long-term employment for his sister's son, she will be eternally grateful to him and possibly take up Totó's position against their brother.

Gaines makes his predictable nightly arrival and weaves his way between the congregated forces of Scopa enthusiasts, exchanging pleasantries as he goes. He reaches the stairs where Totó has strategically positioned himself and his partner, the Signorina, in convenient introduction range to Claudio.

The young man makes a good first impression, shakes Gaines' hand with a firm grip while looking him in the eye and flashing a beautiful smile. Gaines is cordial. Since Claudio doesn't speak English, Uncle Totó does the interpreting. Gaines makes no commitment and tells Claudio to fill out an application for employment and that if he has the qualifications they need, his application will be processed through the proper channels.

At that point Totó interjects, "Now, Gaines! Let's just do this the Italian way."

Gaines ignores Totó's suggestion, thinking that too many unqualified people are on the payroll now for "doing it the Italian way." Once a person is hired, they have a job for life. According to Italian law, even if by some chance a person happens to get fired, the company is obligated to pay a percentage of the salary. As a result of this absurdity, hardly anyone is let go.

14

There is a mystery in this house!" I say, as I take another sip of hot coffee. Gaines doesn't show any interest in my manufactured intrigue this early and sits with his attention fixed on the morning news, or perhaps it is the big blue-eyed newscaster, Maria Grazia. "Bobby Gregory says she's so pretty that he finds it difficult to get ready for work in the morning." At the end of each paragraph she reads, she says 'bene' (bay nay) and bats her baby blues at the camera."

"Mystery? What mystery?"

"Well, Totó is absent. Gone! He is simply *non c'é* (not there). I haven't been pestered by him in three days! He's never in the courtyard working in the flowers and herbs, hanging on the gate, or calling for Briginella to come down! I believe she is beginning to miss him."

"Come to think of it, I haven't seen him either. He's always out when I come in from work."

After saying our goodbyes, I return to il nido, switch off the television, and tidy up our bedroom. That gnawing, lonely feeling grips me. What will I do with myself today until Gaines returns, I wonder. Conscientiously rejecting the luxury of self-pity, I open the French doors in the bath off our bedroom. With much difficulty I try to push open the shutters with the aid of my right foot kicking against the swollen panel until it gives way. The swath of morning light embraces me, thus making my somewhat low spirits soar as I step onto a small, square-shaped, enclosed stone balcony.

Resting my elbows on the cool ledge, I enjoy viewing the local color to the rear of our building. Caged canaries are singing on the back balcony of the house behind the small orange and lemon grove. Directly in front of me about four meters from the balcony is a solitary stone structure that is two-stories high. I am able from the third-floor to gaze down on the seventeenth-century mottled stone. A flue duct is in the corner of the isolated room and is sculpted with two layers of a circular fruit wreath resting on the flat-topped, Mediterranean roof.

The aroma from the decorative chimney is permeating the atmosphere, seducing every living creature within the range of scent, creating a yearning in me for an invitation to Signora Bruno's to partake of that sauce on some type of pasta. It is common knowledge that the Signora prefers to use her outside kitchen instead of the one inside the house because she does not like to have her home filled with cooking odor. That's okay, Signora, I think. You can perfume my balcony with your succulent sugo anytime!

I notice Signora Bruno outside, washing vegetables at a small sink next to the back French doors of her house. The large rooftop terrace is brimming full of potted plants, flowers, herbs, shrubs, small trees, and statuary. They were placed by someone who obviously possesses an experienced eye for design, giving the open space charm and interest. The terrace is surrounded by a four-foot high stone enclosure. It continues on with a narrow walkway arriving at the outside, trapezium-shaped kitchen which is supported by the Signorina's back bedroom below.

Often times the Bruno family dine on their lovely terrace, enjoying the well-prepared food, each other's company, and opera music coming from a small cassette recorder. The common ritual of mealtime gives pleasure and enriches our lives. It seems that as Italians, the Bruno family succeeds in renewing this occasion each day without tedium.

I survey the enduring artifacts. The dolmen chimney pots consist of two upright pieces of flat, narrow, cut stone positioned on end. They are parallel on top of the flue, allowing space for the smoke to escape. It is capped by a square-cut piece topped off by a stone shaped cone resembling whimsical, crudely made

Cortile with plants.

hats. The contrivances are as functional today as when they were fabricated in the seventeenth century.

It would be fun to paint this, I think. I wish I could do it. "Let's go out and buy some oils, Bridgie."

"Now." The redhead responds wildly wagging her tail.

"Sì, sì! Right now." I laugh.

Stefania is moseying around in the courtyard looking disinterestedly at the plant life. In the corner of the cortile she takes hold of one of the large leaves of the gigantic rubber tree plant which grows against the Signorina's house next door, making a privacy wall three stories high. The fine powdery film of paint residue dusted the leaves enough for Stefania to write her name on the large piece of foliage.

As Bridget and I descend the outside stairs, the masculine voice of the one who has been invisible in recent days is heard reprimanding the teenage girl from within the house. "Find something to do. You're bloody idle today." Stefania gives a disrespectful flip of her hand from under her chin toward his direction to indicate that she has no intention of following his suggestion.

The dog yields to her instinct of controlling the descent by placing her mouth over my instep until the movement is accomplished with one foot. She repetitiously acts out the sequence with the other foot. Stefania watches as I descend.

"She has an incessant urge to herd me."

Stefania smiles at us, draws close to the steps, and places her hands on each side of Briginella's red head. "Ciao, bella mia," says Stefania, as she kisses the top knot on the dog's lovely, soft head and strokes her admiringly.

"No school today?"

The large girl motions with her index finger extended from a clinched fist moving rapidly from side to side. This action coincides with a cluck of her tongue, puckered lips, and head nodding from side to side. She then switches from gesturing to verbalizing, "*Sciopero oggi.*" (Strike today.)

"What are you all disenchanted about now?"

100

"Well," she says in her deliberate British accent, which displays all the forbearance of England's female prime minister, "The excuse is protesting nuclear energy plants, but the real reason is that it's spring and everyone is tired of school and the teachers' authority. There is going to be a demonstration at Piazza St. Oronzo at *mezzogiorno* (noon)."

"Would you like to go to an art store with me? It's not far, just down by St. Matthew's."

"Sure," she says excitedly. "Just give me a moment to change and tell Dad."

We stroll through the picturesque streets turning left off via Palmieri onto Corso Vittorio Emanuele II, walking toward Piazza St. Oronzo. Everytime I go out I discover new things and today is no exception. When I gaze ahead and see the Palazzo Personè-Tafuri with Neoclassical linearity, I notice for the first time a corner balcony that is magnificently supported by seventeen caryatids which are sculpted Baroque horses and sheep.

There are times when we are driven flush with the walls by scooters and indifferent motorists. Some are celebrating their freedom from the classroom and, unfortunately, others know no other way to get from one place to another without endangering unsuspecting pedestrians.

We turn right passing Piazza Vittorio Emanuele and continue to follow the narrowing passages toward Porto Sainto Biago, another sixteenth century gate.

The shop borders the street before we come to St Matthew's. "It's a good thing this door opens in, Stefania!"

"I should say! Let's get in before we get clipped."

Following my customary tendency, I check out the vaulted ceiling first. It is dingy with decades of accumulated dust and layers of grime which are highlighted by gossamer threads spun into intricate snares. Apart from the obvious need for a good cleaning, I find what is always searched for in these antiquated caves. There is no disappointment here, only pure treasure.

101

The arches are shrouded in diminished cerulean blue and accentuated by rolling, suspended cloud forms which are attended by gowned cherubs dancing in the heavens and carrying floral cascades of roses and swags of greenery tied together with ribbon and embellished by trailing streamers.

We stretch back our heads, delighting in the newly found artistic jewel. "Oh, Stef! I'd gladly put up scaffolding and clean the whole thing myself just to see the veil of the ages lifted so the beauty as no one has seen it in this century could shine through."

The octogenarian proprietor enters our sphere of admiration, smiles up at the ceiling and volunteers proudly, *"Mio nonno."* (My grandfather.)

"Bellisimo!" I respond. Reluctant to re-enter the present, I tell the shop owner that I have come for some tubes of artists oils.

He positions himself behind the stacks of piled clutter on the countertop and picks up the Windsor-Newton chart of colors. Holding the chart so I can see it, he waits eagerly for my order.

"Vorrei giallo, rosso, verde e azzuro." (I would like yellow, red, green and blue.)

"Aspeta, Signora! Adesso. Il giallo, il numero diciasette." (Wait, Mrs., now yellow, number seventeen.) He holds out his hand restraining me from giving him the remainder of my order. He turns around and commences to put his stiffened, bony framework onto the wooden ladder which is attached to the top shelf by two small metal wheels set into a groove, enabling him to glide around the meters of shelving which line the walls.

An inconspicuous elderly gentleman is seated next to the wall beside the end of the counter. He repeats the order in a decrepit voice, *"Il Giallo, il numero diciasette, la pace."* (Yellow, number seventeen, the peace.)

I turn to him with mild curiosity and he gives me a snaggle-toothed grin and begins to swing his crossed leg.

The proprietor awkwardly moves his brittle bones from the ladder and places the tube on the counter. His bright, greyish-green eyes pierce me while he waits for my next commission. *"Rosso."* He squints at the chart moving a little closer and says, *"Il Rosso, il numero venti-sei."* (Red, number twenty-six.)

His seated companion pipes up, *"Il rosso, il numero venti-sei é una zingara che é chiaroveggente."* (Gypsy, that is the astrologer.) He displays a bit more lightheartedness and gives a kick to his swinging leg.

I am puzzled by his little performance everytime I order a color.

The shopkeeper has made his pickup and is unsteadily negotiating the ladder for the second time. Stefania and I are holding our breath, watching his every move and praying he makes it to the floor without falling. He places the red tube uniformly next to the yellow and looks to me for his next bid.

Reluctantly acquiescing to his regulated mode of operation, I decide to give up any further plans of accomplishment this morning because I know that by the time he fills my order of the next six tubes, it will be time for il pranzo and the other shops will be closed. I say. *"Verde, undici."* (Green, number eleven.)

"Ah! *Sì, sì, sì, sì, sì, Il verde, il numero undici."*

We simultaneously look toward the old chap who delights in the attention and voices. *"Il Verde, il numero undici é una trappola per topi!"* (Green, number eleven is a mouse trap.)

I am still confused, but nevertheless amused by his strange ritualistic performance and turn to Stefania, who is laughing so hard that water has flooded her eyes and is spilling down her cheeks and onto her new black T-shirt. She gains control after going through two tissues and attempts to explain to me what the old chap is saying. "The old people of Italy are well-versed in *The Book of Dreams*, which is a dictionary of sorts. You see, every number has an assigned object or vice versa and that is what he is reciting. Every time he hears a number, he tells what it represents in the book. He probably has it all memorized."

"Why is it called a dream book?"

"Well, if you have a dream which has some significance to you or your family, then you can use the numbers of the objects in the dream."

"Use the numbers for what?"

"*Il Lotto.*"

"Oh!" I howl. "The lottery!"

"Yes, it's amazing how many people believe in it. My dad believes it."

"I'll bet he does," I laugh. "Well, does he ever win?"

"Naw."

"I had no idea that it was going to take so long to purchase eight tubes of oils. First we had to order the desired color one at a time."

"Then came the announcement of the number," says Stefania.

"And, let's not forget the tottery climb to the upper regions which were some fifteen feet above."

"And the old man deciphering the numbers into objects."

"Oh! And the quivery return to the floor with one little tube of paint. There were times I didn't think he was going to make it."

"My dad has a dream book. Would you like to see it?"

"I'd love to. Speaking of Totó, where has he been keeping himself the past few days?"

"Oh! Dad's working at the hospital now, sitting at night with a patient so he's been sleeping days."

"Oh Stef, let's take a few minutes to go inside St. Matthew's."

It is an unusual superb building with the concave/convex facade. As far as its style is concerned, it is a triumph of curvilinear architectural lines and a masterpiece of volumic balance. Built at the end of the seventeenth century, it has been called a pantheon of Lecce Baroque. Inside we see statues of the Apostles in the supple Leccese stone, a painting of St. Oronzo, and a fresco of St. Mary of Light. There is a painting of the

Angel with the Torch on the High Altar. It is votive offering from the people of Lecce for the protection from the plague given them by the Virgin of Light.

15

I look at my calendar and notice that today is March Fifth. I start counting the number of days we have been here but am distracted by the echoing sounds of a lock click and the clanging of the metal gate. I hear sixteen toenails meeting the hard surface of the cortile, stairs and marble flooring which are generated by quattro zampe. She is scampering down the hall into the kitchen followed by enthusiastic crunching of masticating jaws, devouring a four minute egg on toast from her stainless steel bowl. This amplified activity replaces all of the muffled and muted movement that goes unnoticed in a stone-free environment. Lecce has had digital sound for centuries, I think, pouring my first cup of coffee upstairs in il nido.

Gaines and I found it necessary to devise a diet for Bridget because the dog food we saw was too high in fat content. Lunch for her is a small tin of tuna and the third meal is two cups of pet puffed rice and a can of beans.

Gaines takes two steps at a time, materializing slightly out of breath. "I have good news and I have bad news! The good news is Bridget did her business and a bit of a wee."

"And the bad news?" I ask, looking up at him.

"The bad news is that there is an empty space where I parked the car last night."

"What?" I quickly set down my cup and saucer. "Perhaps you forgot where you parked it last night."

"I wish. Well, the blocca-sterzo was obviously a waste of time and money."

"What should we do? Call the police?"

"Let's walk to the Questura (police station). It's only a short distance, and I'm sure there will be numerous reports to fill out. You know how Italians like their *documenti*!"

As we near the courtyard, Totó swings open his door and steps outside with a serious searching expression. "Everything okay?"

"The car was stolen last night," Gaines responds.

"Oh no!"

Sofia and Stefania come outside wearing pitiful expressions. "We're so sorry," Sofia states. "Toe, you go to the Questura with them."

"Well, if you likes, I will."

"Thanks, but we will go and try our best. If we get into something we can't handle, Adrianne will come for you."

"Very well then. You leave the dog here, and we'll see to her."

"Thanks, Totó. Now if she becomes a nuisance, I left the key in the door. Just put her inside."

As we leave the gate, we can hear Sofia say, "Jesus, Mary and Joseph!"

"We've been here seven weeks and three days, Gaines. Acquired a phone but lost a car."

"Well, the company makes cars every day. Thank the Lord they give us ours, but I hate it that our beautiful car was stolen."

The small station is only a three minute walk from the apartment, but we are told the car thefts must be reported at the main Questura.

"It only took twelve minutes to get here!" I comment, as we enter the huge marble building. We report the theft and the officer in charge is most helpful and surprisingly organized. When we return home, Gaines phones an Italian colleague who drives him out to the plant, and it is arranged for him to receive another vehicle.

Discarding any thought of a blocca-sterzo as a security measure this time, we rent the only available space in a nearby

107

building, which is used as a garage. One should not confuse this place with what would ordinarily be thought of as a place of business with convenience, order, and efficient management. We have instant realization that this is just another exercise in "see if you can get used to this situation," as it is not even remotely connected to what a lucid or rational person's idea of a rental garage would be. The place is a two-minute walk from the apartment through the historic stone works and has some irksome distractions among the fascinating gargoyles and statuary at St. Teresa's corner. Across the side street from the church is a butcher shop and from within its walls on an early morning it is a common occurrence to hear the last squall of a small animal. This is intensified by a window showcase exhibiting fresh viscera of every form, shape, color, and size hanging on huge steel hooks that allow the drips of fresh blood to be absorbed on paper toweling below the vivid display.

The pigeons have found a home to their liking on the side of St. Teresa's that obviously serves their purpose very well. As a result, their elimination has provided a thick coating on the stone below which forces pedestrians into the precarious path of the demon-possessed motorists. The nauseating route is the first gouge of the spur each day which causes Gaines to yearn for clean streets, and grass and that far away day of finalization of his three-year contract. The second gouge on an early morning is facing the seventeenth-century, cathedral-ceilinged cavern jokingly referred to as "the garage."

"Bram Stoker surely got his inspiration from this place!" I declare. Valerio is the manager. In addition to renting spaces in the structure for long or short-term parking, he also does car washing, oil changing, and minor repairs. He is no rocket scientist but is clever enough not to show up until after Gaines leaves. Thus Gaines himself has to back five cars out of the L-shaped mausoleum to get to his own car and return the others.

Valerio releases his creative frustrations by spray painting designs of potted flowers on the dingy walls. He adds clever little notices under each piece of his work, such as *"Non Tocca I*

108

Fiori!" (Please don't touch the flowers!) He is casual not only in his management style but also in his dress, which is usually swimming trunks, tank-top, and thongs.

The final annoyance occurs each evening when Gaines returns, parks in his assigned space (the last one in this rat-infested chamber), and has to hurry to beat the light before it goes off on a timer. The cost of this aggravation is seventy thousand lire a month, approximately sixty-five dollars. It is surmised that a portion of it goes to Don Corleone's second cousin, but who cares? It is the best insurance in town.

Raho Palazzo with the sculpted profiles.

16

The two-minute walk from our gate to the walled-in villa belonging to the Del'Aquila family is amidst layers of surface grime and aged dinginess masking the elegant, old tonedwellings.

I am oblivious to the defacing scars brought on mostly by the necessities of modern living which sadden the overall appearance. I feast on all the treasures of my centro storico neighborhood. The discoveries I make are invariably remarkable, such as the beautiful woman's profile which was sculpted on each side of the carriage doors of the Raho Palazzo. I wonder who she was. Did a real person inspire the sculptor or owner of the palazzo or was the face from the artists's imagination?

My eyes dance from the fanlights over the doors to partially opened carriage doors and the tranquil, clean settings of courtyards filled with plants, fountains, sculpture, and pampered cats luxuriating in the palatial settings. When one crosses the threshold, it is like leaving filth and chaos to pristine tranquility, trading *inferno* for *paradiso*.

I approach the huge, dark green, oval-topped carriage doors, press the buzzer and smile into the camera. While waiting for the diminutive aperture for pedestrians in the portal to be released, I admire the red bougainvillea peaking shyly over the stone fortification. The towering wall gives me an idea of what it is like to be Lilliputian. I hear the click and step over the ten-inch baseboard, entering another world. Walking under the arched porte-co-chere, I face the three-storied palazzo about twenty meters ahead.

Intricate layers from the past to the present are represented. The single-lane, paved drive is enhanced on each side by ten alternately placed stone pillars supporting clay vessels

Front and inside views of the *Del'Aquila Villa*.

of geraniums and other annuals that spill over the top in a blaze of various colors and pungent aromas.

To my left I notice randomly planted orange and lemon trees and beyond the smallish orchard is a vaulted columned portico stretching the length of the privacy wall. It is the architectural remains of a once-cloistered convent. The ecclesiastical remains give a serene mystical dimension to the setting.

As I walk toward the house, I am serenaded by birds, a luxury in this enclosed retreat. On the right I look at an incline leading to an area which is foliated with plantings of trees, palms, and bushes. A hammock sways leisurely in the gentle breeze. I observe a preserved treehouse resting in the strong limbs of a deep-rooted hardy acacia. Knotted ropes hang idly weathering. The three children and their playmates abandoned the tree house long ago for more grown-up activity at the university in Florence.

A wooden cellar door faces the house, leading to darkened rooms deep under the hillside thicket of play. Another artifact from the Chietri Order (Cloistered Nuns 1505) is an elegant well which is positioned near the house. I gaze upward at the weathered and faded salmon-colored stone villa built in the 1830s by the great-grandfather of Leonardo Del'Aquila. The convent had been closed in 1809 when Giuseppe Bonaparte, King of Spain, decreed all religious orders to be put down.

Suddenly the white, twelve-paned, single French door bursts open. Out comes the volatile Luciana. She is tall, slim, and definitely Mediterranean in looks with grey-green eyes, delicate features and dark hair. She commences to scold me for not taking the liberty of letting myself in. Little does she suspect that I have been nourished aesthetically ever since I set foot on the grounds. As we enter the foyer, our playful banter is reminiscent of two chirpy birds.

The stone-floored area is deluged with all sorts of outer wear and hats orderly placed on hooks. Umbrellas, canes, and riding crops fill the brass urn-shaped umbrella holders. There are beveled mirrors for checking one's appearance and bare table

113

tops yield space for parcels, purses, and mail. The walls are treated in a bright, grass green; and moldings are cleverly done in *faux d'oeil* (fool the eye), accenting the glorious vaulted ceiling.

"Who does this artform, Luciana?" I ask, admiringly looking at the false mouldings.

"An elderly gentleman here in Lecce. He is the only one left who knows the art. Oh! I must tell you! My maid, that completely stupid girl, tried to clean it one day. I was fearful she would rub it off." Luciana starts to lead the way up the circular, stone staircase. She gestures with extended hands and exclaims. "She is completely stupid."

We sit in a cheerful, intimate room at the head of the staircase. "Prendi un caffè?" (Will you take coffee?)

"Certo, grazie."

As I wait for Luciana's return with the tray, I look up at the high ceiling with the sculpted medallion surrounding the hanging chandelier and admire the elaborate ornamentation of the baroque molding.

"*Il caffè é comodo, carico e caldo.* You must learn this, Adrianne. Coffee is to be good, rich and hot."

"*Va bene. comodo, carico e caldo.*"

"Brava."

"*Come si dice* (how do say) in American?" Luciana touches a tall plant placed in front of the French doors.

"Oh! That is a fiddle-back fig, Luciana. We speak English; we don't refer to it as American. Even though our accent is unlike the British people and we probably use more slang, the language that we speak is English."

"Sorry, I stand corrected. You must teach me, Adrianne."

"Sì, Luciana! And you have your work cut out for you if you are going to teach me to speak Italian. Your English is ten times better than my Italian."

"I have my work cut out for me," Luciana puzzles. "What does that mean?"

"It means you have a tough job ahead of you if you are going to teach me your language."

"Why do you want to learn it?" Italia is the only place you can speak it! Why do you bother?"

"Because I believe it is the most beautiful language I've ever heard. And besides, Luciana, I don't want to live here and be unable to understand anything or express myself. There are very few people who speak English in this town. Of course, a lot of them rely on the dialect instead of Tuscan Italian too."

"*Pronti?*" (Ready?) Luciana is smiling at me.

"Sì." I take a small book from my purse entitled *La Storia di Peter Coniglio* (*The Tale of Peter Rabbit*) and begin to read . "*Una volta quattro piccoli conigli che si chiamavano Flopsy, Mopsy, Cottontail e Peter. Si precipitó allora nel capanno per gli attrezzi e salto' inn... inn... inn... inn... a.*"

"*Scusa pronuncia innaffiatoio.*"

"*Grazie In now fiatoh.*"

"*Senti* (listen) *Inafeeatoyyeoh.*"

"What a word *Inafeeatoyyeoh.*"

"*Va be, come se dice in Inglese?*"

I smile. "Watering can."

"Watering can?"

"Sì, not as beautiful as *in-a-fee-a* or whatever."

"*innaffiatoio ripeti.*"

"Oh! *Innaffiatoio. La tua lingua é molto difficile!*" (Your language is very difficult!)

Time passes quickly for our language session and I look at my watch. "I must leave. I have to shop before everything closes. You will come to my house on Friday?"

"Sì, sì! Oh. Adrianne! Aspetta un momento."

Luciana leaves the room and returns with a bouquet of bright yellow flowers on top of a box.

"*Che cos'é ?*" (What is it?)

"This is for you. In Italia we celebrate the Day of the *Donna* on March Eighth and that is today. We give these flowers or a dessert both are called mimosa to lady friends or sisters or our mother and also to daughters. You can keep the mimosa dessert boxed in the refrigerator because it is made mostly of whipped cream with *liquore*, crushed pineapple and pudding on top of *pan di spagna*, a type of sponge cake, and then covered with more whipped cream and formed into a dome. Enjoy."

"Grazie. I'm sure we will. See you at my house on *venerdi sera alle cinque*" (Friday afternoon at five.)

"Va bene."

Another significance of the Day of the Donna is realized as I walk home. My arms are throbbing as I turn the corner and see "the Signorina gargoyle" keeping watch in her front entrance some fifty meters ahead. A motor is started, so I pause beside the driveway which is next to the furniture shop.

Maurizo is out in front helping his papa strip an *Inginocchiatoio* (personal kneeling bench). I am intrigued with the unusual piece of furniture and abandon my attention to the coming auto which is slowly moving in front of my path. My attention is shifted back to the vehicle and its occupants, who are the prostitutes that live above Pasquale's shop. Never having been this close to them before and in the daylight I become puzzled and an uncomfortable feeling comes over me.

One of their friends is coming down the drive way wearing hot pink toreador pants, stiletto heels, and a pale pink off-the-shoulder, tightly stretched long sleeve blouse. She is toting a picnic hamper and a huge bouquet of bright yellow mimosa tied with a deep purple bow. What a sight, my eyes follow this person to the waiting car. Suddenly, the facts hit me like a ton of bricks. I look over to Maurizo, who is observing me attentively hoping I have made the discovery. I mouth the word *"uomini?"* (men) to him. He shakes his head "yes" with amusement.

The car backs out enough to turn and drives away perhaps to the beach or the countryside for a picnic. The bouquet of mimosa has been laid in the back window of the

116

BumBom boy's (transvestites) balcony.

vehicle an artistic display of the flower dedicated to the Day of the Woman.

Totó walks up behind me, but I'm lost in thought, thinking of the car's occupants. He reaches for the boxed dessert and comments with the cigarette still attached to his lips. "Well, it's the Day of the Donna," he says mockingly, as he nods toward the car that has disappeared from sight.

"I can't believe it!" I say, shaking my head.

"What can't you believe?"

"Well, those people are our neighbors! I've never known anyone like them before. Not that I do now exactly. But to see them every day living this close!

We pass the parallelogram-shaped furniture shop, and I glance back over my left shoulder. Checking out the transvestites' little side balcony in the rear has become a habit because their lacy, sexy, freshly laundered lingerie is hung out every morning.

"They have prettier lingerie than I do."

"Well, a girl has to make a living."

"But, they aren't girls, Totó!"

"Ah, sì! We call 'em bum-bom boys. Why Gianfranco has even had breast surgery."

"Oh, for heavens sake! Speaking of making a living, Totó, I understand you are working nights at the hospital."

"Oh! I was sitting up with Francesca's grandfather at the hospital, but not anymore I'm not. I fell asleep last night, the old bloke fell out of bed and they sacked me!"

I stifle the urge to laugh and step behind him as he unlocks the gate so he won't notice my obvious discomfort.

118

17

Today is March Ninth, and I have been invited by Alessandra Grimaldi, *per il caffé dopo il riposo* (coffee after rest), before she and Giovanni go to their shop for the evening trade. I'm beginning to enjoy my social life here very much because I am not restricted to one particular group as the natives obviously are. Luciana, an aristocrat and Alassandra, an educated professional, wouldn't think of socializing with Totó and Sofia, and for that matter, maybe not each other. But I'm an American and the caste rules of hereditary social classes don't seem to apply to me and for that I'm very thankful. The things I enjoy with Luciana and Alessandra are alien to our neighbors and vice-a-versa. I realize how fortunate I am in being able to cross these social barriers.

I enjoy the stroll through the vacant streets, as Lecce has not yet stirred from its afternoon nap. I take in all the Old World flavor of the Charles V period. Lacy balconies of wrought iron display all sorts of motifs. The various themes and swarms of sculpted caryatids supporting balconies hold my interest, as well as the family crests positioned over the huge carriage portals. Before crossing the narrow street, I pause to admire the handsome, wooden, oval-topped doors which lead the way to Alessandra's penthouse.

The only other human stirring in sight is a teenager on a motor scooter stopped at the corner entrance of the Piazza Duomo, some ten meters from me. Since he has seen me as well, I initiate the crossing. Suddenly, triggered by the revving motor and peripheral vision, I recognize my terrible fate. He's going to hit me is my last thought.

Gradually emerging from a stunned state, I have no knowledge of how much time has elapsed. I am powerless by the inhumane trespass. Fleeting spasms of reality shift in blurred forms and colors before my eyes. I sense muffled chatter and then have a brief realization that I'm sprawled on an impenetrable surface.

As the second hand moves from one digit to the next, my awareness is now intensified a bit. My concentration has the capability of focusing on a single thought for no longer than a split second. My vision reflects several pairs of shoes smeared on the stone and my hearing indicates the conversation is no longer edgeless. In fact, it contains all of the lyrical reverberations that have become familiar to me these past eight weeks. Voices are repeating, "Signora," and are followed by a verbal commotion anxious for a response from me.

Finding a source of strength, I gaze past the dimmed faces to a sculpted stone statue of St. Irene supporting a church on her left hand and arm. She is housed in a niche high above on the second story of an edifice. At this time my vision shifts keenly into focus. Realizing that the treasured artifact had escaped my notice before, I feel pleased to finally make its discovery. A sharpened blade of ice is being applied under my kneesock on the inside of my left leg where the front tire had made contact. I am assisted by good samaritans and eventually am able to stand up.

"Oh, *cara, come va?*" (Dear, how are you?)

I turn and recognize Alessandra. *"Non lo so."* (I don't know.)

Suggestions are made about a trip to the hospital for x-rays or at least a visit to a physician's office, but I reject all such notions. Then my attention comes to rest on the appropriately black-attired demon, still astraddle his weapon displaying a sullen, detached demeanor.

Stark reality is making its way to the forefront of my consciousness. I am helpless, stifled, and unequipped to verbalize my outrage at the driver. I'm ignorant of legal rights and whether or not I have any at all. I can say and do nothing, but feel the results of his violation.

"Alessandra, come home with me."

"*Certo, cara mia,*" says Alessandra comforting me. Then to the youth she yells, "*Questa é una brutta situazione. Il ragazzo é cattivo. Tu sei molto cattivo!*" (This is an ugly situation. The boy is mean. You are very mean.) The verbalization is accompanied by a gesture the black demon understands well.

By the time we reach the gate, I am beginning to feel the results of being plummeted onto the stone street and agony has found a dwelling place. Alessandra describes the hit to Totó, Sofia and Stefania, who are idling in the courtyard. They become inflamed. Totó makes a hasty departure after giving instructions to Sofia and Stefania.

Sofia commences to rant, rave, and pace in the cortile, seasoning her harangue with gestures which are a bonafide language of their own. The wild tirade is done in Sofiaese, a blending of the local dialect, a smattering of English and a little pure Tuscany Italian. The unreserved passion is incomprehensible to me and Alessandra.

By now Sofia has managed to work herself into a glorious state of frenzy, which she relishes almost as much as her daily wine and pasta. She continues her passionate outburst against the youth, the local government, the present mayor, and the Archbishop, whom she despises and blames for everything that has gone wrong in her own life since returning from England. Sofia has just about run down when she catches sight of me, as I have not moved since entering the courtyard. My face betrays my suffering. Sofia asks, "*Fai mi volere a faccia the spirits, me darlin'?*" (Do you want me to give you a massage?)

"I don't know what you're asking, Sofia, but I hurt so bad that I don't care what you do to me. And if it is extreme unction you're suggesting, yes, I think I might need it!"

121

The women help me up the stairs. They strip me down to my slip, and Sofia's strong, massive hands doused with rubbing alcohol massage the aching leg which now sports a lemon-sized knot where the scooter hit. The massaging sends me into wails of anguish, but the experience of the masseuse dictates to never let up the kneading. She simply reiterates her apologies each time contact is made. "*Mi dispiace*, me darlin'. (I'm sorry.)

I begin to realize what a friend I have in Sofia and her family. My tears are not only for the pain I'm in, but they are mixed with tears of a thankful heart.

The next morning I drowsily step down into il nido where Gaines is seated on the sofa, dressed for the office, and watching the news, which is interspersed with cereal munching and coffee sipping.

"How do you feel?"

"Oh, okay, I guess. At least I don't hurt anymore."

"Let me see your knee."

I extend my leg from under my robe. "Hey, Gaines! The knot is gone!"

"Ah! But look between your toes where the blood has settled. Boy! Sofia simply rubbed that knot out of you! Doesn't it hurt you to walk?"

"Not a bit."

"Well, you take it easy today. If you feel up to it, we have Italian class tonight. We're all going out to eat afterwards *senza* Whitecotton. No one wants to be around him any longer than they have to."

"I wish we had a better teacher, Gaines."

"Yes, I know! It's disappointing." He bends over to kiss me goodbye. "I believe that we need to start praying that God will give us a mental toughness. Life is especially difficult here and we aren't used to it."

"That is an excellent idea."

"Bridgie, you be a good girl and take care of Mom."

The dog wags her tail and accompanies him to the door.

122

This evening we meet our American colleagues at Piazza St. Oronzo and walk through the dimly lit, sleazy alleyway past the two houses of ill repute and toward the language studio.

"Tonight 'Cottonmouth' wants us to know the subjunctive mood," Bobby says, seeming a little worried.

"Not only the present, but the imperfect!" Adds Margie.

"Shoot, kids! I just learned the word for toilet paper the other day! I'm sure not ready for this!"

"None of us are ready for this tense," Norma responds. "Why, we haven't even studied the past participles yet!"

Chet removes his pipe and offers, "It's better to humiliate us this way. He seems to have it in for us Americans."

"Well, I don't think an Englishman should be teaching us Italian anyway. We need to be hearing the language from a native. It doesn't show very good judgement on the company's part," adds Tom.

Wearing dismal expressions, we reluctantly trudge up the grandiose marble staircase.

Gaines whispers to Bobby, "We should be back on exercise fifteen."

"Tell me about it!"

After class is over, Whitecotton directs his overbearing remarks to me. "I heard you were run down yesterday by a kid on a motor scooter."

"Yes, I was."

"Well what are you going to do about it?"

"What can I do?"

"Get your witnesses and sue the bloody hell out of the no-good bastard. I've done it! By law you can take away everything his parents own."

"Oh, really?"

The others have left the classroom as Norma and I gather up our materials and walk toward the door. We pass Whitecotton's desk. He says to me, "This is what I think, when I think of you." He shoves a white pad of paper with his freshly

123

scrawled memo on it. I read his salacious thoughts and without giving him the slightest notice walk out with Norma.

"Did you read what he wrote me?"

"Yes, I did!"

"This is the last time I'll come to his class!"

Everyone's mood has lightened up considerably upon conclusion of the class, and we walk across the Piazza to Guido e Figli for dinner.

"We're really chic tonight. It's nine in the evening, and we're just now dining," Gaines says.

"I'd rather be a little less chic, Gaines, and eat no later than six!" Responds Margie.

Chet proposes our customary toast, "If we were all there, we wouldn't be here."

"Here, here," we respond clicking our glasses.

18

As well as satisfying my aesthetic tastes, the abundance of opulent Baroque architecture is a treasure to my sight. It reaches into the recesses of my soul each time I leave the protective enclosure of the cortile and progress through the narrow passages of this seventeenth-century city.

The historic district is vast and cannot be known in a week, in a month, or even in a year. It is sadly draped in an imposing shroud of mourning brought on by the pollution of our modern age. Nevertheless, Lecce bears this encumbrance with dignity and patience while waiting for that day when her brilliance will shine through restoration. While marking time, Lecce lends her remarkably designed structures to preoccupied folk caught up in the restricting net of daily demands.

I am awestruck with the craftsmanship of the artisans who slavishly devoted their lives to urging, prodding, and enticing the hidden forms of cherubs, fruit, floral wreaths, and caryatids (as well as the ever present mystifying gargoyles) to come forth from the local limestone, exposing the intricate likenesses to all passersby. What kind of genius knew the figures were concealed and could coax them into view fascinates me. I relentlessly seize glances upward while side-stepping the heavy traffic of cars, motor scooters, bicycles, pedestrians, and the recurring deposits of dog droppings. My intention is to become well acquainted with every single sculpted piece that embellishes, adorns, and enriches the once naked Renaissance facades of my new neighborhood.

I meet Maurizo, who is stripping the old finish from a carved wooden door, supported by two sawhorses in front of the entrance of his father's shop. He looks up as I near him in the

Partial view of front gate.

street, and a smile spreads across his handsome face as he gives his habitual, accelerated salutation, "Salvi, ciao, buon giorno." "Ciao, Maurizo," I say, smiling back, but quicken my pace as my front gate comes partially into view. I am in an agony of my own making the weighty plastic shopping bags feel as though they are cutting my fingers to the bone. If only I had taken the shopping cart with me this morning, I think regrettably. In the distance a feminine voice can be heard intermittently calling "Signora." Assuming the beckon is directed at one of the natives, I am unmindful of all the quotidian cacophony of a busy morning in the quarter--the shrill annoyance of power tools inside a house being restored, ladies chattering about the annual tax on television sets, il postino's, bell on the handlebars of his scooter activated each time a delivery is made; and the fruttivendolo chanting his morning's produce, *"Cipolle, pomodori, cicorie, rape e barbabietole."* (Onions, tomatoes, chicory, wild broccoli, and leafy green tops of beets.)

"Signora, Signora," the woman summons, trying to catch up with me. Finally, I turn to face my determined assailant, who is slightly out of breath and is offering me a small, folded piece of paper. I welcome almost any kind of fraternization in these socially sparse, "new kid on the block" days. I smile at the stranger and lower my throbbing appendages until the burden comes to rest on the stone street. Reaching for the note with stiffened, curled claws, I try rheumatically to unfold the white piece of paper. The stranger asks, *"Che significa?"* (What does it mean?) as she points to the message that she herself has delivered.

The familiar expression is hand printed and it is in English, piercing me as I read to myself: "It was bound to happen sooner or later!" I am perplexed by the obvious innuendo, I soberly search the face of this stranger. Who is she and what does she want? Who took the trouble to send this to me? Perhaps it is only a coincidence: hopefully that's all it is. I prefer that thought and proceed to interpret the well-known English phrase to the young woman. The delivery mission is accomplished and the Italian's departure is as efficient as her arrival. I am bewildered and look on as the stranger disappears around the corner. Contemplating the incident as I stoop to grasp the ridged plastic loops with a little more suppleness now that the blood has had a chance to reach the fingertips, there is no awareness of that physical rejuvenation for my thoughts have been abducted by the obscure, puzzling message inducing a trancelike movement for the remaining few meters to my security gate. Negotiating the lock and stepping downward, I give the swinging iron frame a little kick of my heel causing a clanging sound as it slams shut behind me.

I drift into the cortile, finding some comfort in a bamboo chair with a faded chintz cushion. I become part of the tranquil setting of potted greenery, involuntarily soothed by inhaling the vegetal perfumery of geranium, carnation, and basil housed in the antiquated, moss-laden clay pots.

The curious brief encounter and note have overshadowed all thoughts, stifling previously made plans for the day, which are not so pressing now as I enter a state of reflection over the past week. I look down at the opened note on my lap. I read it again: "It was bound to happen sooner or later!" Is it referring to the car theft? Or, is it a reference to my getting knocked down the other day by the kid on the scooter? It has to be someone who knows English well to use a phrase like that. Is it someone's cruel way of gloating about our recent discouragements? Perhaps it is because we don't belong here and never will. Both incidents occurred within five days' time. Whoever wrote the note took the trouble to have it delivered to me. I can't believe that any of the Americans would stoop to that sort of mischief. Whitecotton comes to mind, certainly a prime suspect. He loves to taunt, and it is second nature for him to humiliate someone.

"Here, try this." A plate is shoved under my nose. The golden brown rice ball smells so good to me. "Careful, it's bloody hot!" Totó stands in front of me waiting for his morsel to be tasted.

128

Cortile.

I pick it up and bite into the crusty ball. It is embedded with pieces of ham and melted mozzarella cheese. It was rolled in seasoned bread crumbs and fried in light, extra virgin olive oil. "This is delicious, Totó!"

"Well, I saw you looked a little peaked, like, when you came in. Here, have some Copertino." He hands me a glass of the local red wine he has just poured from a large plastic container which is always stored in the compartment under the stairs. "You'll feel better, like, after you eat a bite and have a glass of vino. It will cure what's ailing you."

I take the glass. All of a sudden, the tears well up. I begin fighting them back.

He senses my need to be alone and says, "Oh, bloody hell! I've got to tend to my cooking. Sofia will let the rest of them bloody balls burn if I'm not in there supervising, like." He runs into the house shouting in the dialect to poor Sofia.

I grin, knowing full well that Sofia never lets anything burn. I tuck the note in the side pocket of my skirt and finish the rice ball which will be lunch today. Maybe there are spiteful people out there who are watching and waiting for our stumbles and misfortunes. But God certainly has blessed us with this wonderful family always doing and caring for us.

Bridget runs out from Sofia's front room and nudges her snout into my lap. "I'll bet you've already had a treat!" Bridget sits, gazing into my eyes, almost smiling at me. "*Tu sei molto contenta, no? Bella mia.*" (You are very happy.) I hug her, still fighting the weepiness.

*

It is time for Bridgie's last outing of the evening. I volunteer for duty although it is a mission that Gaines usually undertakes. The street is quiet but well-lighted at this hour. I have nothing to fear with my dog at my side. Even though Bridget was not with me when I was hit by the kid on the motor scooter, the dog aggressively initiates attacks on all persons who are unfortunate enough to be astraddle a scooter and come within

130

range of her powerful jaws. Bridget has taken up my defense, and war is waged on all cyclists.

Responsibility for protection and security of Via dei Sepolcri Messapici within a specifically defined area known only to Bridget has been assumed by her. Innocent people are scrutinized and oftentimes come under serious threat for reasons known only to quattro zampe. Both Totó and I have been laid low on the stone streets of Lecce in an effort to hold the overzealous, powerfully energized canine during an offensive charge.

This evening Bridget executes her call to nature without delay and starts toward the gate which is within eyeshot. The quietude is disrupted by an inebriated songster escalating in volume as he clumsily negotiates the corner. I recognize the pathetic old soul. He is a well known figure who has an artistic reputation. Discovering he is not alone, he commences to speak as he comes near me. Bridget begins to lunge, growl, and threaten.

I use all of my strength to hold the dog and am fearful of slipping on the polished, well-worn stones. My stress level soars, plus the fact that I'm concerned about what the drunk will do next. But he seems to be happy and displays joy and ease in his delusive state. He exhibits a distorted smile and utters delirious gibberish.

I strain to speak loudly over Bridget's racket and say, "*Io non capisco. Io sono Americana!*" (I do not understand. I am an American.) He throws his head back and launches a rowdy belly laugh, and as he staggers by me he says in perfect English, "Okay, bye-bye Baby," and gives me a wave of his hand singing as he saunters on through the picturesque passageway.

Gaines appears at the gate and I loosen Bridgie so she can run to him. "I had a feeling I should come down here. Is everything all right?"

I start to laugh with relief, nodding my head yes. My strength has been drained as I walk to the gate, wondering if my weakened knees will support me.

chiesa di San Matteo

Part II

Nothing is the Same Anymore

19

It is Saturday and Gaines is happy to be away from the office today and tomorrow.

"Adrianne, the power just went off. What do you have on?" Gaines yells to me from the bathroom. "I'm trying to use my hair dryer!"

"Oh! Gaines, I'm running the dishwasher and I just turned on the oven. I'll switch off the oven for now and restore the power!" I hurry down the stairs, turn off the oven and go into the guest room to switch on the circuit breaker. I wait a few minutes for Gaines to finish drying his hair and turn the oven on again, hoping the roast will be done for il pranzo.

I go up to slip into my dress and check my make-up, where I find a disgruntled, frowning husband in il nido. He holds out the tedious chore of removing the off-white string stitched in roman numerals between the belt loops at the waist of his trousers. Gaines has no patience for this sort of activity and in exasperation exclaims, "Oh, this is ridiculous!"

"Here, let me have it! Sit down there and have another cup of coffee." I take the trousers and the small scissors in the Swiss army knife from Gaines and clip the string from the waistband of the recently cleaned garment.

"In some ways the twentieth century hasn't arrived in Lecce. At home, One Hour Martinizing pins colored tabs of numbered paper to the clothing. Here it is someone's job to handstitch the numbers into each piece, in roman numerals no less. It's rather quaint, don't you think?"

"I don't find it as engrossing as you do."

"Yesterday when I picked up the cleaning, the owner left her ironing board to wait on me. They don't even have a steam press. She started to remove your trousers from the hanger and fold them up. She had the shop's wrapping paper rolled out and ready to tear off when I realized what she was doing. I let her know that I prefer the clothes to be left on the hangers. She thought it a strange idea, informing me that everyone prefers their clothes folded and wrapped in the shop's signature paper. I told her that I didn't want to press the clothes again before they could be worn. Then she wrote out my receipt and asked if I would allow her to record a lower amount than it actually was while declaring that her taxes are too high already."

"Well, what can one expect in a place where salt and stamps are sold at the tobacco store, hum?" Gaines chuckles, shaking his head.

"Or in a place where it takes weeks to have new heels put on your shoes. I'm going downstairs to check on the dinner, and then I'll be ready to go with you to the shoe repair."

Having followed Totó's vague directions to the shoe repair, Gaines and I have our doubts, going purely by appearance because the establishment is void of any identifying marks. There is no sign over the entrance or bold block lettering on the front window or door, as other shopkeepers proudly display.

"It appears to be closed," I say, standing as near as I dare to the grimy front window and peering inside while shielding my eyes from the brightness of the morning's light. "I do see a light on, Gaines. One needs x-ray vision to get through the grime on this window. It hasn't been washed since the eighteenth century. Oh, where is Clark Kent when we need him?" Glancing down I see the first evidence that this is indeed the place. On the inside of the window, where most shop owners display attractive collages of their work, is a pile of assorted, misshapen, worn-out, and outdated shoes.

Gaines tries the door knob. "It's open!"

We hesitantly move inside. There is no hint of activity behind the counter of the dimly lit room, no belts buzzing, none of the familiar scents associated with shoe leather, rubber heels, and polish. Instead, the shop reeks of dust and stench from the moisture collected in the stone as well as stale, cheap tobacco, and foot odor from piles of well-worn shoes. The air is too stifling for deep breathing.

We hear a chair move on the grimy marble flooring. Following the sound, we see four men playing a card game seated as close to another window as space permits. Rising from the table, and still holding his cards, a tiny man walks toward us. We deduce that he must be the proprietor because his appearance announces that he sure enough belongs here.

He hasn't shaved for a few days, and he looks as if he has slept in his clothes for a week. Rings of grime around his neck have soiled the top of his underwear shirt.

He uses the familiar opening line of the local shopkeepers, "*Dimmi!*" (Tell me.)

Gaines starts to describe the shoes and before he can finish, the Italiano starts looking in unmarked plastic bags, paper sacks, and cardboard boxes. He pulls out a drawer and rummages through it. Finally he says, "*Eccoli*" (here they are) and lifts the shoes for Gaines to see, announcing, "They aren't ready!"

Gaines has evaluated the situation and concludes it is hopeless.

"They have been here for a month and I need them. When can you get to it?" Gaines asks facetiously, nudging me with his elbow.

The bedraggled shoe repairman says, "What's your hurry? It's spring now! People are wearing white and light-colored shoes. Black shoes are for fall and winter."

The remark is so absurd coming from one who isn't even acquainted with soap and water let alone aware of fashion trends that Gaines, who is a good bit taller, reaches for the shoes, secures them, and says, "Buon giorno, signore."

Relieved to be outside, Gaines and I inhale the polluted exhaust fumes and entertain ourselves by recounting the past several minutes.

Arriving home, we find Totó bent over a perforated ring-shaped aluminum container. He is wearing his rubber boots from the morning's outing to the country. Looking into the pail, Gaines and I see it is working alive with the fruits of Totó's morning labor. The iridescent pinkish-grey spiral shaped shells are home for the small, slimy snails. Their long, headless necks sport two prominent antennae above a pair of protruding eyes. There is an earth odor coming from the pail as we watch them sluggishly creep around on top of one another and up the metal sides, progressing only so far, losing their grip, and crashing down on the others. They make a clacking sound when their shells come in contact.

Totó is busy preparing the aluminum ring for their new housing. "They will live in here for two weeks, like, and I'll feed them a diet of bread crumbs and lettuce or some greens. That cleans them out, and then they'll be ready to eat." He looks at Gaines. "Will you eat the *lumàche*?" (Snails?)

Without hesitation, Gaines emphatically says, "No!"

Totó grins mischievously and asks me.

"I'll try one."

Totó inserts a glass bowl into the center ring, confining the new inhabitants. "Now, I'll leave them here for the cleaning-out time."

"You mean to leave them out here in the middle of the courtyard to walk around every time we come in and go out?" I ask.

Totó enjoys the nuisance he has created and chuckles.

The snails must need daylight, I conclude, knowing that Totó will never give a logical explanation for anything he does, so I dismiss it.

We enter the house and Gaines turns to me with his hand on the back of his neck.

" I hate to tell you this, Adrianne, but I have been feeling ill all morning. I think I have a fever."

136

"I'll call Domenica and have her help me call the physician that has been assigned to us. I put his number by the phone the other day."

Two hours later I lead the doctor into the bedroom, where Gaines is shivering under the covers. *Il Dottore* sets his handsome leather case on the floor next to the bed, takes out his stethoscope, listens, and thumps around on Gaines' chest. He asks if he can borrow a fever thermometer, and keeping the results to himself gives Gaines an injection and me two prescriptions.

I hurry up to the Farmacia to have them filled. The druggist informs me that I can buy syringes at the grocery store.

"Syringes? I don't want syringes, just give me the pills."

"Impossibile, Signora."

"*Perche*?" (Why?)

"Molto cara."

I return to the courtyard with a thirty day supply of syringes, medicine, alcohol, and cotton. I meet Totó and the Signorina stooped over the snails.

"Nothing is easy here, Totó."

"Like what?" he asks, as he places bread crumbs in the round container.

"Like this idiotic situation as a perfect example. Now I have to find someone to give Gaines injections on the weekends. During the week he can get them from the nurse at the plant."

"Oh, there's lots of people around here who gives the shots, like."

Annoyed at his vague nonchalance, "And who is that, pray tell? And how much does that cost? The pharmacist told me injections are cheaper than the pills. I don't see how it could be. You have to buy the medicine, buy the syringes, as well as cotton and alcohol, and then pay someone to give the bloody shots. Everything is so unbelievably inconvenient here. Nothing is easy!"

"*Calma, stai tranquila.* (Calm down.) You're gettin' yourself all upset, like," he says breaking up the lettuce and putting it into the container.

"Well, whom do you suggest I get for the weekend injections?"

"Oh, there's this one here," looking at the Signorina. "And there's that one over there," nodding toward Domenica's. "If you can trust her, that is."

*

On Monday evening Gaines arrives home at his predictable time and is very amused. "Adrianne, you know that Arab that lives down there by the furniture shop next to the transvestites? He came up to me in the street just now, introduced himself, and said, 'My name is Omar Iscabar,' or something that sounded like that. Then he said, 'I understand you're sick and receiving injections.' I was flabbergasted! Talk about a grapevine! Then he said, ' I've just been to the doctor, and I need to find someone to give me the injections too! Who did you get?' "

"We have no privacy at all, Gaines."

Every Saturday and Sunday afternoon for a month Gaines and Domenica rendezvous at the marble-top table in the dining room, where Gaines drops his jeans and undershorts. Domenica shows me the strategic point on his cheek where the needle is inserted. Afterwards we have caffé, which is also under Domenica's tutelage.

20

It is March 16 and all seven of us Americans as well as Briginella have been in captivity for two months. Finally, the work visas arrive, enabling us like civilized people to discard the encumbrance of money pouches and open bank accounts. We are to meet at the bank at ten this morning to sign signature cards and meet the bank officer that has been assigned to us because he speaks English.

Before I go to the bank, I'm going to pick up a special dessert that I have been advised to buy, which is sold only during the Lenten season, and I have been told to go early because the lines get long during the day. It is only an eight minute walk to the twelfth century Saint Giovanni Evangelista Church. I take a quick look inside because the doors are open, allowing the passersby to become momentary parishioners, lighting candles, praying, saying rosaries briefly, and exiting quietly to continue their morning errands. The beautiful interior is a fine example of the local Baroque.

I walk around the outside of the church and find the adjoining Benedictine Convent. The cloistered order has been in the territory since the twelfth century as well.

The nuns are famous for their dessert of *Pasta di Mandorle* made and sold every Christmas and Easter season. The recipe is finely ground almonds, sugar, chocolate, laced with *amoretto liquore*. It is put in a lamb mold for Easter and fish form for Christmas.

I groan at the sea of humanity that is already flowing out into the parking lot. Queuing is not part of the Italians modus operandi, so it is anyone's guess as to whom one stands behind. Forty minutes later I place my order to the cloistered one who exposes only a dark eye to the outside world behind the one-inch diameter hole in the dumb-waiter. The dessert is ordered by weight and there are two sizes. *Un kilo e mezzo o due kili.* (One-and-a-half kilos or two kilos.) "Vorrei due di due kili, per favore." (I would like two, of the two kilos, please.) I place sixty-thousand lire (about fifty-five dollars) on the lazy Susan, and it is whirled out of sight and immediately the two desserts appear on the circular tray in plain white boxes.

Happy to be outside again, I manage to dodge the mass confusion in the streets of the old city and walk toward modern Lecce because the bank is on the square of Piazza Mazzini.

The glass door locks behind our group, and an identical one leading to the lobby has already locked, thus holding us in the transparent cell until the seated guard within viewing distance releases the lock which frees us from the momentary confinement. It is a useful security measure devised for banks and jewelry stores to discourage modern day Bonnie and Clyde types.

We are escorted to an office, seated on comfortable office furniture, and given a choice of caffé or juice. A young male teller who has command of the English language is introduced to everyone. He is the one who will take care of our banking needs. The officer-in-charge of opening new accounts puts his worst foot forward by making the suggestion that we wives should have written permission from our husbands before being allowed to make a withdrawal from our own accounts!

When this provincial idea finally penetrates those of us whom it most concerns, the room closes in all of a sudden. Brought on by tension and hostility, the contraction increases at such a high rate of speed that one would think a natural disaster is about to take place. The climate has changed quite drastically since the pleasant and warm atmosphere of the beginning of the meeting. The silent, shock-filled protest is so effective that the officer who made the asinine proposal senses from the loathing looks coming his way that he is in "deep do-do" and becomes anxious to forgo the suggestion proceeding to safer and more pertinent subjects.

Fortunately, good news is dispensed. It seems the company has finally gotten around to paying everyone; and the first paychecks have been electronically posted from northern Italy.

We finish their business, part company, and I walk toward the old city. Passing a toy store, I decide to go in and inquire about a jigsaw puzzle. The proprietress speaks English. This is a wonderful birthday, I think.

"What are you doing in Lecce? Are you studying Italian? Where are you from?" She asks all the standard questions.

I tell the clerk that I am from Illinois. The lady jumps on that with much excitement. "Oh, Illinois."

The statement is said with such reverential awe that it causes me to take a step backward and scrutinize this overzealous, high-strung woman. Disbelieving the response, I finally figure that the woman must be a Lincoln buff.

The shopowner reaches beside the cash register. "I always keep it right here," she says, almost caressing the map of Illinois. She has to unfold it only once to expose the capital city which has been highlighted in yellow magic marker.

"Do you know Johnny?"

Hum. It's not ol' Honest Abe that she is enamored with. I repeat, "Johnny?"

"Yes! Johnny Price. He gave me this map. Isn't he wonderful?"

"Oh, sure! I know Johnny. In fact he just returned to Lecce last evening." I leave the shop with a puzzle and amusement brought on by the clerk's fervor for Springfield and especially Johnny Price, recalling the company employee who spends five to six weeks in Lecce about three times a year. Johnny has been on this rawhiding circuit for the past three years. He is a big, robust individual in his late forties, a natural born politician revered and renowned throughout the plant as well as by every Italian in the city who makes his acquaintance.

Johnny stays at the *Risorgimento*, an old hotel in the historic district and always his home while in the city.

All of us are well aware of his popularity and joke about the hotel waving flags on his arrival and draping the establishment in black crepe when he leaves. Johnny loves the social life, which is evidenced by the fact that he has bookings for dinner through future visits. He has confided that his wife is becoming hostile over his increasing tonnage, but he will not disappoint his Italian friends by not fraternizing with them and partaking of every tasty morsel that they put before him, voiced by the encouragement of "*mangi*." (You eat.)

I open the gate and am confronted with a few degrees of reduced temperature induced by the six-inch drop from the street into the stone enclosure. I push the gate to with a motion of my backside because my arms are firmly wrapped around the morning's shopping. Paralysis has set into my clasping fingers.

Hastening to the wider expanse of the courtyard I emerge from under the arched tester embracing the emitting light from the heavens high above. My nostrils are invaded by the vegetal emanation of basil, geranium, carnations, potting soil, and mold, giving an appropriate antiquated attraction to the vessels of terra cotta randomly set next to the stone privacy walls that are discolored by seeping streaks of moss. The offering of perpetual tranquility is indisputably soothing to all who enter with the weariness and exhaustion visited on the participants of the combative effervescence and chaotic lifestyle in the streets of Lecce.

Totó, closely attended by Briginella, is making his way up the stairs, carrying a covered dish with both hands aimed toward the opposite side of the skilled paws and jaws of his self-appointed overseer. Reaching the landing while balancing the object of his mission on his forearm and palm, he carefully negotiates the key now left in the lock for his convenience.

He procures safety for the morning's creative delicacy by placing it on top of the refrigerator, high above the reach of any mammal eighteen inches tall with a leg span of three feet.

Pleased with his timing and never wanting his good deeds to go unnoticed, he gives an uplifted "Buon giorno" to me as I enter the kitchen and rest the packages on the table.

"Oh! It has been a good morning, Totó." I kick off my shoes with a sigh of relief.

"Ya, ya, ya. All them shopkeepers celebrate every time they sees you comin' across the Piazza." In a more serious tone he says, "Now, I made the puree this morning and it turned out okay, like. So I thought you and Gaines could eat it tonight. Cook number four or five spaghetti. With an emphatic slap of his palm on the table, which startles me and emphasizes the seriousness of adherence to his teaching, "But, don't overcook the pasta!" With a transformation to his milder side, he adds, "It's supposed to be al dente, like." Demonstrating this point with the act of biting his teeth together, he says, "To the tooth, as we say!"

Performing an acute observation of the morning's purchases, his beady little eyes dance from the opening of one plastic bag to another.

"You going to work a puzzle?"

I draw out my response, "Yes," amused at his unquenchable curiosity about the most insignificant things of our lives. Acquiescing, I give him a tidbit more. "I'm going to have it out to work on when the caffé group comes after riposo."

Nodding, he tries unsuccessfully to see into the other bags, but they are all concealed by wrapping, thus thwarting his need to know. Totó cares nothing for politics and can't give a date or a name to any of the wealth of history that surrounds him. He fills his storehouse of knowledge with all of the comings and goings of his neighbors. The intricate particulars of our lives is what interests him, plus soccer, about which he is equally passionate. "Do you mind if I go up to see if you can get channel seven, like?"

"Go ahead! Channel five is the only one I care to watch. During riposo they show American films in Italian. I wish they

143

were in English, but I guess it's better for me they aren't. Anyway, it helps pass the time until things start rolling again."

Stepping from the kitchen through the opened French doors in my stocking feet, I wrestle with the beaded *portiero* that hangs on the outside of the doors for the purpose of discouraging flies and mosquitoes from entering the house. Unfortunately it isn't a deterrent for the harmless chameleons who draw me right out of my skin every time I'm confronted with them.

The twelve-foot square, privately enclosed patio is filled with laundry that was hung there earlier this morning. Feeling the clothes for dryness, I wonder why Totó is so interested in channel seven anyway. That is the second time he has mentioned it. Then, dismissing it as another trivial preoccupation of his, I hear him pass the kitchen.

"Ya can't get it," he yells on his way out.

I take the puzzle out of the sack, admire the lovely George Saurat scene on the lid and dump out fifteen-hundred pieces on a large piece of cardboard taken from one of the shipping cartons. I begin turning them right side up, organizing the color groupings and separating the border from the interior pieces.

It is seven-fifteen and Gaines enters the gate. He is enthusiastically greeted by Totó at the foot of the stairway, noticing that he has picked up some sticky yuck on his shoe, he takes a tissue out of his pocket and proceeds to clean it off.

"When ya gets that business taken care of like, stop in here for a minute."

Gaines obliges but is annoyed by the postponement of changing from his suit into the comfort of jeans. After an arduous day of Italian language, Italian management and Italian mentality, he is in no mood for one of Totó's schemes. Entering the front room of the blaring television, which is ignored, Stefania willingly relinquishes her chair to Gaines and excuses herself to do homework.

Sofia doesn't deviate from her usual greeting, "You all right?"

"Ah *sì, sì, Sofia! Non c'é male.*" (Not bad). She pours Gaines a cup of steaming hot espresso and starts to scoop sugar into the diminutive vessel, he cautions, "Just one, Sofia. Thanks!" He smiles and nods to the couple seated on the bamboo settee.

Totó pulls up a chair next to Gaines and giving him a nudge, says, "Now," extending his hand in the couple's direction, "These are the parents of the boy you're supposed to be gettin' a job for."

Gaines chokes on his caffé while trying to stifle his laughter. Thinking that the introduction just made by Totó is by far the most absurd he has ever heard in his life, Gaines rests the cup and saucer on the table in front of him, rises from his chair and extends his right hand to the woman and then to her husband and says, "Gaines Grant."

They shake hands responding *"Piacere,"* (pleased to know you), but never utter their own identities. Of course, Gaines has already concluded that the woman is Totó's sister, Angelina, and the man is her husband, Alfredo.

Totó gives Gaines another nudge and says, "Now, Gaines. Let's just do this business the Italian way, like."

I am seated on the balcony reading, but with very little concentration. I look at my watch and notice it has been thirty minutes since Gaines entered the front room below. When he finally comes upstairs, he looks fatigued and says, "I've got to get out of these clothes. The hard soles are killing me. I'll join you in a minute."

Gaines plops in the bamboo chair with a sigh.

"What was that all about?" I ask pointing to the lower level.

First, he recounts the ludicrous introduction, which shakes us with laughter. "They tried to bribe me into hiring their son, Claudio."

"Really?"

"Yes, when they made the first offer, I was so shocked I couldn't even respond to them. For one thing the offer was as much as that kid would make in his first year. I think they thought I was stalling holding out for more money, because they upped the price. I told them that I don't do business that way. I've suspected how some of the people at the plant have been hired. Now it appears a lot of them are on the payroll because, in Totó's words, they 'do business the Italian way.' "

"What did Totó say when you turned them down?"

"Not a thing. I know he is disappointed. He doesn't understand us. Italians think we're fools to pass up the money."

Tonight we dine on number four spaghetti al dente and the succulent purée *della casa* Pascarella.

"It should be bottled and mass produced!" I say. "Borrowing Totó's words, 'I wouldn't pay anyone to feed me,' either if I could turn out a sauce like this!"

"*Sono buoni.*" (Spaghetti is good.) Chimes Gaines.

21

"It's Friday, *Venerdi*," I proclaim.

"Almost another week down, T.G.I.F." Gaines tips his cup drinking the last drop.

"You going to the big market with Norma?"

"Sì, sì."

"Well, be careful. See you tonight."

"*Altrettanto*." (The same to you.)

The key has been inserted in the lock for Totó's use, as he comes to do the weekly cleaning on Friday mornings. I hear him before he makes the ascension to il nido.

"Can I come up?"

I have the dressing room door latched and respond, "Yes, come ahead." Hesitating because I think I can hear another voice, I reach into the built-in closet for a bag that matches my clothes, check myself in the full-length mirror, open the door and enter il nido where I meet Totó and an unfamiliar face that belongs to the voice I heard before.

The men are standing in front of the television with a toolbox opened on the floor. Totó serves another of his infamous introductions, "This here is the man who has come to fix the tele, like."

"Buon giorno, Signora."

Feigning pleasantness to cover my agitation, I speak to the TV repairman, but give Totó a sharp look coupled with a touch of sarcasm. "I wasn't aware the set needs repairs!"

"Oh, he's goin' to make it so you can get more channels, like."

"Whatever." I resign myself once again to his constant interference. "I'm leaving for Norma's now. Bridgie's lunch, a small tin of tuna, is in her bowl. Give it to her at noon. She is not to have any pasta today. She's getting too fat. Make her mind."

"Ya, ya, ya, ya, ya," is his disinterested response.

As I walk past the kitchen, I slip a cinquemila lire bill under the ring on the tuna lid. Bridget escorts me to the door.

The twenty-five minutes to Norma's is just a nice walk, I reflect. At the Piazza, I meet Greta Von Hoffmeyer, a lady who had been a tour guide for some of the company-sponsored day trips around Puglia. Greta works in Lecce as a language teacher and a court translator. She has been married to an Italian journalist for twenty years.

"How are you coping with life here in Italia, Adrianne?"

"We've encountered a couple of discouraging things, but nothing so major that I've wanted to leave it all and return to the States."

"I see."

"Greta, you've lived with these people in the old city, and even speak the Leccese dialect."

She looks at me, smiling and questions. "Yes?"

"Every day my neighbors ask me, 'What are you going to eat today?' Why do they ask me that? It wouldn't occur to me to ask someone I didn't know very well what they are going to eat. I don't think it is any of their business."

Greta laughs aloud. "I remember being bewildered by that as well many years ago. It's just what they talk about. For instance, I called my mother in Germany the other day. When I hung up the receiver, my husband's first question was 'What did she eat today?' Not, how is her cold? Some cultures are concerned with the weather. Italians are preoccupied with food, soccer, and sex and not necessarily in that order either."

I have to face two menacing intersections en route to casa Browning. Intersections are always a concern to me after the scooter incident. The mere sound of the pesky things send chills and irrational fear within me, but I'm determined to overcome the fear and not let the situation get the better of me.

148

Norma is waiting for me in front of her apartment building when I arrive and we head for the pottery vender. She purchases another piece to add to her growing collection."

"Let's go to the leather goods, Adrianne. I need a new bag for summer."

"Can you find what you want in this pile?"

"Well, there are two that will work, now I have to decide on one. What's that?"

"It's a man's purse sort of a miniature brief case. By unsnapping this shoulder strap and just using the handle, I believe Gaines would carry it."

"Well, I know Tom wouldn't!"

"Gaines is ultraconservative too, but he has been complaining about not having enough space in his briefcase for all the car documents he has to have with him all the time." I examine it closely. "I like it, Norma. If Gaines won't use it, I will!"

"Oh, Adrianne! Look, they have English chintz." We spend a lengthy amount of time looking through the piles of chintz remnants. "Norma, I think I've narrowed it down to these two pieces. They'll go with the color scheme in the apartment and I can use them as throws to protect the loveseats when we're not having company."

I reach to unzip my quilted, cloth bag and to my horror find it unzipped already. The little tapestry bag with my favorite lavender, crocheted-edged handkerchief, Italian identification, International and Illinois driver's licenses and about thirty-thousand lire is gone. "Someone has picked my purse while we were going through the material. Oh, it makes me so angry!"

"Oh, no! How much money did you lose?"

"Not that much, really. Just about twenty-five dollars. But now I have the hassle of getting another ID and drivers' licenses. My favorite little tapestry bag and handkerchief is what I really care about. A friend gave them to me."

"I'll pay for your material, Adrianne. Just try to calm down. It could have been worse."

"Whoever did it is so slick! I wasn't even aware of it!"

"That's their reputation. Now we know why the linen vendor always warns us to keep our bags under our armpits. Let's walk over to Raffaello's for rustici and cappucino."

Norma and I part company after lunch. The streets are being vacated. Il pranzo and riposo is magnetically drawing the populace indoors.

I am feeling drowsiness converge upon me when a carload of young people intrude on my tranquil walk homeward. A display of waving arms and heads of hair parted by the breeze are protruding from the open windows. "*É Tedesca.*" (German.) They call to me in passing.

"No, sono Americana," I yell, and immediately there is a resounding cheer from the carload. A surge of pride gushes through me making me feel all warm and cozy, but it is instantly followed by an intense stinging behind my eyes which are welling up with hot tears. A subconscious truth surfaces with such a bolt that all inner sensibilities are awakened, arousing cognizance of my overwhelming homesickness. The realization surrounds and compresses my psyche prohibiting any denial or escape from the burdensome encumbrance of intense pain.

I hear my own voice finally admitting all the elements of my nostalgia, precisely and coherently identifying each one. "I miss grass. I miss my friends and our times together. I miss sidewalks and clean streets. I miss my country. And, oh how I miss hearing English." All objects have become watery distortions as I make my way home with an accelerated stride.

Suddenly I find myself face to face with Sofia, who is standing at the partially opened gate looking candidly into my soul, questioning, "You all right?"

I step down and into the voluminous arms surrounding my small frame, enveloping me inside the mass of soft warm flesh. I break down in a deluge of tears. "Oh, Sofia! I'm so homesick that I ache!"

Briginella, never wanting to be left out of a hug, runs through the courtyard to the huddle, using her nose as a tool, tries to pry us apart enough to make her own entrance into the comfort.

Feeling as though I have been drenched and rung out, I need the comfort of the sofa in il nido with Bridgie at my feet and a good film to get lost in for awhile to escape the agony of homesickness. I pick up the remote control from the flat-topped, wooden trunk which serves as a coffee table and footstool, turn on the TV to see what film channel five is showing this afternoon, press all the buttons three times, and I make the annoying discovery that channel five has been replaced with channel seven. "Oh, that interfering jerk!" Ugly thoughts surface in my mind. As I close my eyes, I fantasize contacting the local organization and paying them to break Totó's legs or at least work him over real good.

"Are you okay?"

I open my eyes. "Oh, Gaines! I was sleeping so soundly, I didn't hear you come in. Where's Bridgie?"

"She met me at the door and went on down to Totó's. Sofia told me you had a bad day."

"Oh, I'm all right. I suppose a little homesickness never hurt anyone."

The buzzer sounds and we hear Bridgie go into a barking frenzy. "That's Johnny. He walked over from the Risorgimento. He's going to dinner with us Americans tonight because all his other weekends are booked with his Italian friends. We're meeting at Rollo's at eight."

I look at my watch. "Oh, good! I've got time to freshen up."

"I'll take care of Johnny down in the living room."

"*Benvenuto* (Welcome), Johnny!" I say, entering the living room.

"Hello there! It's nice to see you again! You and Gaines have a lovely place here."

"Thanks, we like it."

"Did you loose something today?"

"Why, yes! How do you know?"

Johnny hands me, my Italian ID and Illinois driver's license.

"Where did you get these, Johnny?"

"Some guy walks up to me out at the plant late this afternoon. He asks if I know you. Said his wife and daughter found them on the street this morning."

"Oh, sure! They found them in my purse at the market. Thank you so much, I was dreading the hassle of having to replace them. Tell me, does everyone in town know you, Johnny? Your reputation really doesn't do you justice. You should run for *Síndaco* (Mayor). I bet you would win."

Johnny laughs and says, "I'd like that."

Fusilli ai fegatini (spiral shaped pasta in oil, herbs, and chicken livers) is one of Anna Rollo's specialties. *Penne alla Boscaiola* (quill pen-shaped pasta, tomato based sauce, mushrooms and seasonings) is another. Her minestrone is to die for. Gaines and Bobby have taught her husband, Luigi, to make American style pizza with the onions, but no American pizza can compete with Luigi's crust. Dinner at our favorite Trattoria Del Centro Storico is always a treat, as well as the fellowship with the other Americans on a Friday night. After the day I've had I'm in need of Anna's food for the soul and good company.

Later on, Gaines and I say goodnight to the others and stroll home in the moonlight. Our serenity is interrupted the minute we enter the courtyard. Totó sticks his head out of the door. "Stop here for a little dessert, like."

Seeing him reminds me of the ill will I feel toward him for messing up the channels on the TV. Domenica and Tiziana are also in the front room. The television is blaring as usual. Totó assumes his perch on the side of the little iron bed. Sofia serves *gelato, stracciatella affogato* in San Marzano. (Chocolate chip ice cream sunk in an herbal liqueur of Puglia.) Totó takes the *tele-commando* and switches to another channel and announces with much enthusiasm, "Here it is! It's starting now!"

We stop talking and turn toward the large screen in the corner of the room. A sleazy looking game show host appears and announces, "It's time for *Colpo Grosso*" (Big hit). The burlesque beat of the music begins and a chorus line of very well-endowed, topless, long-legged girls wearing tiny string bikinis dance across the screen bumping and grinding, tossing and twirling tassels fastened to the nipples of their megasized, firm breasts.

Everyone in the room is shocked into silence by the spectacle, except Totó, who leaps from his perch like a frog on a lily pad and commences swinging his hips, weaving in, out and around the seated audience of neighbors. He, too, is bumping and grinding to the suggestive music and proudly announces, "When I was married to Joan Collins, te he he, I won a beautiful legs contest." Totó's eyes follow the screen imitating the routine and flavors it with a commentary of the dancers anatomy. "This one's got nice tits. Now that one has a cute little ass, hey, Gaines?" Never missing a beat, nimbly maneuvering around his seated guests in his Dr. Scholl's sandals, Totó is having the time of his life! "I had a friend come and fix your set this morning, Gaines. Now you can get this program every night on channel seven!" he says, proudly as he sashayes around the room.

I put my foot out to trip him, as he dances by, but he sees the obstruction and nimbly does a side-step. We leave, and as we start up the stairs, Totó follows us outside.

"Now, you doesn't have to pay my friend for fixing the tele, like, but it would be a nice gesture if you'd buy a lottery ticket from him. He's going to have a drawing this summer for a free TV."

"Totó, you had the one station I enjoyed watching replaced with that trash. He's not getting a cent from me!"

Totó giggles. "Gaines likes it! Don't you, Gaines?"

"Buona notte, Totó. I'll switch the channel back for you, Honey. It's a simple thing to do."

22

There is a loud knock on the door. I leave the puzzle table in il nido. "I'll get it, Gaines. It sounds like you know who." I open the door.

Totó steps past me, carrying a covered dish and walks toward the kitchen while barking orders. "Now get yourselves a little red wine and some bread."

"Gaines, come down here!" I call, obeying the orders given.

"Now, sit down here. I'm goin' to show you how to eat the *lumàche*" (snails).

We look at each other in nauseating horror, but without protest, we knuckle under his headship.

"No need for them utensils, you eats these with your fingers." He lifts the lid on the tureen and the steam rolls out of the conchiferous nutrient simmering in Totó's sauce. He confidently spoons hearty servings to our squeamish-selves. "Now, you pick one up with your fingers like this, and ya sucks the meat out of the shell." I feel my stomach executing a summersault.

He pours himself a glass of wine and sits down between us at the square table to oversee the completion of his entree. "Now, if I brought them up here, like, and left the dish, you would have thrown them in the garbage and tomorrow you'd be a tellin' me how good they were."

We laugh at his accurate observation.

"The flavor of the red sauce is very light and delicate. Have you used a meat base and garlic to a little amount of tomato sauce?" I ask.

Totó doesn't respond because he is not about to share his recipe.

Gaines adds, "The snails don't seem to have an offensive taste."

"They seem to take on the flavor of the secret sauce," I say, smiling at Totó.

"If one doesn't like the rubbery texture of the meat that is the worse thing about them," Gaines says.

"They are the texture of chicken gizzards. You also put wine or sherry in that sauce, didn't you?" Totó doesn't answer me.

"When I prepares the lumàche, like, I have to go to the artichoke fields early in the morning, when the snails are feeding on the plants. Then they have to be cleaned out; that takes two weeks on a diet of bread crumbs and greens, and then, I has to make the purée. It's too much bloody work to have it thrown away, like! And besides, you can't come here to Puglia and not try one of the best plates in the whole region." Of course he is right, but I can't agree with him. That will simply give him too much encouragement, and he doesn't need anymore.

"I can't honestly say I've developed a taste for snails," Gaines says, yawning and stretching out on the sofa.

"It's the idea more than anything else. The taste isn't offensive, even for a couple of Midwesterners."

"The rubbery texture might turn some people off."

I return to the puzzle-table, studying it with some curiosity. "I can't believe this."

"What can't you believe?"

"I knew there was something wrong with this picture when I passed it this morning."

"Like what?"

"Someone has forced the pieces into the spaces. The colors are off and the pieces don't fit. This entire section has to be reworked! Unbelievable!"

"Oh! Italians! They force, push, press and feed everyone and everything to bend to their will."

155

23

This morning I look in my closet and examine each dress as I move them across the rod. I'm trying to decide on the most appropriate outfit for the Red Cross Benefit this evening, thinking that all *L'Italiane* will be decked out in black.

Margie and I have been invited to the lavish affair by the president of the local chapter, Flavia Rainaldi. The cost for dinner at the Governor's Palace and a chance to see a world class ballerina, Carla Fracci, dance is one-hundred-fifty-thousand lire ($135.)

I begin to press the dress selected, when I hear that familiar knock. I open the door and attempt to say, "Come in," but Totó steps past me going toward the kitchen before I can utter a word. He places a covered dish on top of the refrigerator for safe keeping. I stand in the empty threshold and say, "Please come in. Oh, thank you very much. I will." I close the door drawing a deep breath.

"Well, what are we going to be force-fed today, *anguilla?*" (eel.)

He gives no notice. "Now, I made some *pasta con piselli freschi* (fresh peas with pasta.) It turned out nice, like. So I thought you and Gaines would enjoy some tonight."

"That is very thoughtful of you, Totó. Gaines will enjoy it, I'm sure."

He looks at me with an inquiring, searching expression. Anticipating an explanation of my plans for the evening, he stands motionless staring at me. "Well, it won't be good tomorrow, like," he utters while examining my face for some response. This unexplained tidbit has aroused his inquisitive streak so acutely that he can't imagine it because he knows that in the evening we never part company. He has no other excuse to stay, so he makes an abrupt departure.

I return to pressing the dress and have been here just long enough for the iron to become warm again, when I hear the knock at the door.

"Oh, *lasciami in pace!*" (Leave me in peace!) I say, aloud.

I open the door expecting another swift intrusion past me, but instead I find Totó positioning the morning's mail on the window sill, standing the envelopes evenly upright. He looks at me and motions to his little display. "There's the mail. You got nothing but bills today. My gas bill is too high. Next month I'm changing the numbers on that bloody meter down there!"

"I hear Italian prisons are so forbidding that people really try to stay out of them."

"Oh, that's just *pubblicità*. Why, you get a free tele and a woman every two or three months. What more could a bloke want?"

"What indeed?" I laugh.

"Now! Why don't you join us for watermelon this evening? It's the *Signorina's Onomàstico*" (Saint's Day.)

"Thanks, I'll tell Gaines! He'll probably join you all for a while."

He decides to fish a little. "Well, if you wants to go to the Piazza for something, Stefania could go with you, like, for the company."

I find it difficult to cloak my amusement, but decide, the torment should continue. "Oh, Totó, I left the iron on, I must go see about it, excuse me."

Reluctantly, he says, "*Sì, ci vediamo.*" (We'll see each other.)

A loud knock arouses me from my nap on the sofa. "Oh, I wish he would get a job!" I open the door and a large bouquet of pungent white blossoms are pushed in my face thus changing my frown to a grin. "Thank you, Totó!" After putting them in water, I look out at the next-door neighbor's garden, and see the bush where the bouquet had grown.

At eight o'clock Margie and I arrive at the Palace.

"Kid, there sure are a lot of people here. Isn't this exciting?"

"Oh, Margie! Look at the ushers!" They are elaborately dressed in powdered wigs, white gloves and seventeenth-century costumes in keeping with the architecture and furnishings of the palace.

Flavia sees us when we enter and comes to greet us. "Hi! Come with me! I want you to meet the Governor and his wife before you go into the grand ballroom for the performance."

We are seated and the performance begins with the master of ceremonies a middle-aged man who is also in charge of the ballet company. He is wearing a designer tuxedo in an unusual dove color. The jacket is of topcoat length and dramatically draped around his shoulders. At one point in his tedious dissertation of the dance, he flamboyantly flings it to the stage floor for an affect. Margie nudges me. "He is something else! I wish he'd just shut up and let her dance!"

After Carla's performance, the crowd is ushered into a large reception room. I look at my watch. "No wonder I'm so hungry, Margie. It's eleven-thirty!"

"Kid, I had a good little snack at five o'clock."

"I haven't eaten since noon!"

The waiters move through the crowd in pairs opening a series of eight double doors exposing the elegant buffet. The creme da le creme of Lecce converge on the buffet like hogs to the trough. We are parted by the rolling tide of the famished crowd. The last I see of Margie, who can usually hold her own anywhere, is being moved along the table's edge in the opposite direction. She's filling her plate as fast as time allows. I am moved in another crest toward the other end of the table. Everyone in the crowd is talking and there is so much commotion it is difficult to think straight. I find food in abundance, but no time for a thoughtful selection. The pasta dishes interest me and

I try several different types. The shrimp looks very good. There is lamb, beef, turkey and pork. I sample the lamb because the natives are well known for their excellent preparation of it. When the tide of humanity ebbs and we meet again, we start laughing and say in unison, "What did you get?" We look at each other's plates for comparison. Both our plates are piled high.

Seating is found with Flavia's parents, whom we know casually. As the evening progresses, many platters of food make the rounds and no one goes home hungry.

Flavia's father is an oriental rug merchant from Turkey. He initiates some conversation.

"Do you play bridge?" he asks. "We are always looking for extra players."

Margie and I aren't interested in playing and he goes on to another interest which is films. "I especially like James Dean," he volunteers.

We discuss Dean's films.

"Do you miss living outside of your country?" I inquire.

"Yes, but I have to be near my grandchildren. Flavia has two daughters. Beatrice is sixteen and Tosca is thirteen."

I invite Flavia and her mother to visit me tomorrow after riposo and we say goodnight to those seated at our table.

"I learned one important thing tonight, Margie."

"What's that, kid?"

"Italians don't queue up to eat!"

When I return home Gaines wakes up.

"Totó was mighty curious about where you went tonight."

"I was really spiteful today, I wouldn't tell him where I was going. You should have seen him." I laugh. "He couldn't stand not knowing. It was a little revenge on my part because he wouldn't part with his sauce recipe for the snails."

"I told him where you went and he made a comment about how bloody expensive it must have been. And then he had the audacity to say that since we are going back to the States for

August, we had better watch our spending so we would have the money to go."

"I told him I had taken care of us for twenty-eight years without any help from anyone."

24

The next day I hear the bell on the postman's scooter and so does Totó. I can see him heading for the box. He scrutinizes each piece of mail and brings mine up the stairs, placing the envelopes on edge in the windowsill.

I give him time to disappear and quietly ease the double swing type window inside and reach for the letters. "Hum, a letter from Fernanda. I wonder what she wants." I attempt to read the squiggly italicized style, but decide it's just too laborious to decipher the handwriting and go up to il nido with a book by Jane Austen for riposo.

The sound of Sofia's voice calling, "Adriana, Adriana," from the courtyard awakens me. I drowsily open the French doors and peer down. Sofia says, "Come on down for caffé."

"Okay! Briginella, want to go down to Sofia's?" The dog is off the sofa and making her way to the front door before I can get my shoes on. Bridgie runs ahead, slaps their partially ajar door with her paw and hears the enthusiastic sounds of welcome.

Stefania carries the tray supporting the steaming brew seducing everyone in the room. *"Che profumo"* (Smells good), I say, before taking my first sip. *"Comodo, carico e caldo. È in buona compagnia."* (The coffee is good, rich and hot. With good company.)

"Your Italian is getting better, Adrianne, " volunteers Stefania.

"Grazie molto." (Thanks very much.)

Totó downs his caffé and turns his attention to me. "I see ya got a letter from Bologna today."

That statement causes me to choke on the caffè. I commence coughing and laughing simultaneously.

He is looking intently from his perched position on the side of the day bed, as is Sofia from her chair. They silently wait for me to divulge news of the one they love to hate most.

I am amused because I couldn't read Fernanda's squiggles and can't honestly tell them a thing. "Well, if Fernanda wants to tell us something important, she should send a message by Alessandra. Gaines and I have tremendous difficulty reading her handwriting."

"Stefania can help you out, like. She has become used to the way they write." Stefania shoots Totó a very dark look. She is embarrassed by his snoopy streak and involving her in his schemes.

I decide to be generous with *i vicini oggi* (the neighbors, today). "I'll get the letter."

Stefania turns to Totó saying. "You old nosey parker!"

The girl pulls the folded pages from the envelope and begins to translate aloud in her lovely, precise English accent. "Dear Mr. and Mrs. Grant, I hope you are both very well. I send my best to you." Sofia groans at that and rolls back her eyes.

"I have just returned from visiting my children in school in your beautiful country."

Totó stiffens himself, uttering his disapproval. "Oh, that bloody bitch!"

"Dad, keep your opinions to yourself."

"Go on, go on." Totó waves his hand at her.

"It will be necessary for me to raise your rent from." Stefania drifts off in disbelief as she discovers the amount.

I believe the girl is going to faint. Sofia and Totó are mesmerized on the edge of their seats, realizing that they are finally going to know how much rent we are paying.

Stefania recovers slightly and repeats, "It will be necessary for me to raise your rent from *un milione al mese* to un *milione due-cento al mese.*"

162

Totó springs from the day bed as if he has been ejected and puts his face so close to me that I move backward. "You're paying that bloody, stuck-up bitch *un milione* a month for that place up there?" He shakes with rage.

I am thoroughly enjoying the little drama for the day and casually shake my head saying, "yes."

"Madonna!" exclaims Sofia, placing her hand on her large bosom adding, "Jesus, Mary and Joseph!"

Stefania sits speechless, while Sofia rises, shaking her hands and bellowing, "*ladra, ladra, ladra* (thief.) Moving her tonnage around the room, she prepares for another of her famous harangues.

Totó points his finger in my face. "You can't pay her another bloody cent," he proclaims with total authority.

"Listen, un milione is about eight-hundred dollars with today's exchange rate. It really isn't all that expensive for a beautiful, spacious apartment. If we had been sent to Chicago instead, our rent would have been a lot more."

They haven't heard a word, nor do they want to. This bit of information enables them to get wonderfully worked up and hate Fernanda all the more. Sofia sashayes from one end of the room to the other. "*Lei é tremenda.*" (She is awful.)

Totó is going out the door toward the gate. He turns and says, "I'll find you another place to live."

"I don't want another place to live, and neither does Gaines or Bridget! Do you, Bridgie?"

The dog raises her head off the floor and voices, "Now."

This antic brings Stefania out of her stupor, laughing with me at the dog's response.

Totó steps outside the gate, turns around almost running and bursts into the front room announcing, "Oh, hell! It's the bloody priest! He's comin' here right now, like."

"What? What is he talking about?"

"The priest comes every year to bless all the houses in the neighborhood. He'll want to bless yours as well," answers Stefania.

163

"That's okay, Stef. But what is the procedure?"

Sofia says, "We'll come up with him. *Tu non hai bisogno di fare niente!*" (You don't have to do anything.)

"Ha! She'll have to give him a little something," Totó interjects. He gestures by rubbing his thumb and fingers together. "And don't give him any more than *cinquemila*" ($4.)

The "bloody priest" enters the house dressed in a plain white alb carrying an unlit censer and prayer book. He is attended by Totó, Sofia and Stefania wearing sanctimonious expressions, quite a change from moments earlier. Bridgie takes a liking to the priest and sits very close to his feet and rests her head against his gown during the ceremony and prayer.

When I share my day with Gaines, he explains, "Well, Bridgie is Irish Catholic, not a protestant like us."

"You've really lost it, Gaines. This place has finally driven you over the edge."

"You are probably right. After a day of struggling with the language and the people, I'm weary. When we go home I'm going to make a sign to hang in our house and it will say, NO "*INI*" SPOKEN HERE!"

"I love it!"

25

Bobby Gregory has a kitchenette in his hotel apartment and enjoys cooking, but chili is his speciality, referred to as dog food by one Italian. He does his weekly shopping at Standa on Saturday mornings.

There is a false sense of ease and anonymity when an outsider enters the largest food chain in the city. One can feign being a normal person even though complexion and clothing style state otherwise. We can actually browse the aisles, selecting conveniently prepackaged goods within an arm's reach and never have to betray our amateur language status, if we choose.

Bobby possesses a private, sensitive nature and feels comfortable in a larger setting rather than becoming the spectacle of the one-owner shops where foreigners are forced to converse, divulge, dance and declare personal information such as, "Why are you in Lecce? How long? Where do you live? How much rent do you pay?"

This particular Saturday Bobby is gliding through the aisles, tossing weekly needs into his cart when he hears that oh-so-familiar, melodious female voice ringing. The voice that eternally soars above any other sound whether it is normal conversation, a child's crying or the commotion of a jackhammer. Margie's clear-cut, well-defined cords are recognizable anywhere. The large woman or grande donna as the Italians affectionately refer to her is in the produce section, chiming a mispronounced request which is sending shoppers in the vicinity into snickers and creating a mass exodus in the surrounding area.

Bobby hears her blunder from the next aisle over and is hoping she will pipe down. He eases up behind her. "Margie, Margie! Hush up! Don't say that word!"

165

Turning to him, "Bobby, hi! Why don't Eyetalians eat figs? Is it against their religion or something? Honestly, they are the most superstitious people I have ever seen."

"You aren't asking for figs, Margie. You're asking if they have pussy!"

"Oh!" She throws back her head and peels with laughter. Bobby's embarrassment is eased and he is able to enjoy the mistake as well.

"Well, how in the heck do you say "fig" in Eyetalian anyway?"

"*Figa*, not *fica!*"

Chet comes from another part of the store wearing his neat, well-pressed classic style of clothing and puts a can of charcoal starter and a sack of briquettes into the cart. Taking the pipe from his mouth, he smiles and greets Bobby. "Why don't you come out for a beer this afternoon? We can even take a walk on the beach. It's so nice out today."

It is commonly felt among us Americans that shopping at Standa is more like home until the dreaded task of paying the checker arrives. The girls of the gestapo are indistinguishable. They are all demon-possessed and take a demented pleasure in the art of humiliating middle-aged Americans not yet familiar with various denominations of bills and coins. There is unanimous agreement that the check-out girls manifest the most detestable, odious, loathsome behavior ever encountered in a collective group of humans. They scold, rebuke, snarl, and demand the correct change claiming never to have a supply of coins. There is a strong consensus among *gli Americani* that the checkers don't possess the grey matter it takes to cipher!

While standing in line the Robsons have girded their loins, applied garlic and enough thought to bring a sum of change sufficient to meet the need. Chet notices the total amount of their morning's purchase displayed on the electronic screen. While puffing thoughtfully on his pipe, he reaches for his wallet and opens it revealing impeccably arranged bills. He takes some out and lays them on the counter. Finding he needs another five

166

thousand lire, he proceeds to return to his wallet looking for a five at which time the pushy, impatient clerk spies one and reaches into his opened wallet. Chet is overcome with anger. Every ounce of his mild manner has fled and is being taken over with rage dynamically surging to the surface. He grips her hand of impropriety and picks up the bills on the counter plus the one inside his wallet and thrusts them into her grasp. Taking his pipe in hand, he points it in her astounded face and pierces her with his Nordic blue eyes. Chet fledges her with such a "come-uppance," said solely in English, yet his meaning does not escape her comprehension that she cannot utter an "*ini!*"

View of the *cortile* to terrace and wasp nest.

26

Bridget's period of adjustment is disquieting for me and Gaines to witness and has been more prolonged than we ever imagined. Does a dog sob in her sleep? On two occasions she awakened us with what sounded like sobbing in her slumber. Her insecurities were such that for the first four months she would not leave our side unless it was to visit her friends downstairs for goodies.

Finally her confidence has returned and now she indulges herself daily with a morning's snooze in the sun on the rooftop terrace all by herself. I catch a glimpse of her lovely, auburn coat, highlighted by the sunlight, from il nido. I walk along the railed catwalk and go up the four steps to join Bridgie, who acknowledges me with half-opened eyes and three lazy wags of her tail.

Stepping onto the terrace, I become the target of an aggressive air strike by three highly threatened and antagonized wasps. There is no time for recourse and instantly I feel intense smarting stings under my right eye and on both arms. Fleeing the scene, I stumble down the steps, and rush into my boudoir with Nurse Goodpuppy in attendance. In thirty minutes, my eye is swollen shut and the welts on each arm are blistered and holding clear bubbles filled with a watery substance.

I answer the loud knock at the door and face Totó, who is clasping a heavy, plastic carton full of glass water bottles and is accompanied by Stefania.

Totó exclaims, "Oh, no!"

"You poor thing," says Stefania.

It isn't long until the covey has been informed of the wasp assault. This brings Tiziana and Mamma Domenica, self-appointed medical overseer, to me with the same determination equal to what the flying foes had managed earlier. Before knowing it, I'm being led by Tiziana out of the courtyard and up the street to a doctor. Entering the crowded waiting room it is apparent some people have been here long enough to become fatigued. Tiziana is not disconcerted one iota by the situation.

I manage to loosen her grip on my hand, but it is snatched up again as Tiziana leads me to the receptionist's window. She pulls me close to the opening for the nurse to see my pathetic face. While standing in front of the access door into the doctor's office, rapid-fire Leccese dialect is exchanged amongst Tiziana, the nurse and the curious involving themselves in the business of others.

The door is opened and Tiziana bounds through, yanking my arm. Tiziana introduces me to the doctor who resembles a Las Vegas lounge lizard in his vivid, printed, silk shirt which is opened to the fourth button, displaying thick, dark ringlets in the V-shaped opening. Nestled amongst the woolly unsanitary mass of curly filaments are graduating lengths of gold chains, one bearing a massive crucifix. I focus on the cross, but my qualms unfortunately are not eased.

The doctor, never moving from his finely upholstered leather chair, writes out a prescription. We are out of there and on our way to the pharmacy on the corner before one can say, "That's socialized medicine!"

I am already well-acquainted with the three neighborhood pharmacists. This pharmacy has early frescos with illustrations on the lower part of the steep, vaulted ceiling. The subjects are sixteenth-century chemists mirroring a Danteesque likeness. Early apothecary accessories are displayed and prevalent diseases of the time are listed. The business's Grecian origin is prominently publicized on the walls.

The youngest of the partners displays a pristine professionalism. He reads the prescription and gives my wounds a studied gaze. *"Signora, devo dirle che questa medicina é molta cara."* (I must inform you that this medication is very expensive.)

"*Quanto costa?*" (How much?) Tiziana asks.

"*Novantacinque mila lire*" (approximately $85.)

"Madonna!" she wails, slapping her hand on the counter. This leads Tiziana into a wild tirade in the local dialect. Unperturbed, the pharmacist shrugs. I am skeptical toward the medic and his prescription. "*Vorrei parlarne con mio marito, quando lui ritornerá stasera.*" (I would like to discuss with my husband when he returns this evening.)

The druggist nods in agreement, giving me the impression that he too is doubtful.

Gaines and I plan to meet our friends at Rollo's. Looking into the make-up mirror, I decide that my eye must be covered. Using a white styrofoam cup, I cut a small section off the bottom and around one side to make an acceptable convex patch. A little clear tape holds the patch in position over my flesh-impacted eye. Stefania and Tiziana think the white patch looks most bewitching and, create their own eye-patches to sport this evening in the courtyard for cards and *chiacchiere* (gossip.)

Gaines finds the wasp nest, which is concealed under a pipe close to the entrance steps of the terrace. He douses their snug retreat with a bucket of water and forces it to the floor. The eight residents which are home at the time meet their demise under his foot.

Balcony furnished for summer.

27

The next evening Domenica and Tiziana bustle into the courtyard arena, discharging their usual amount of unreserved, animated energy. Uprooting all tranquility, they wrench everyone's attention to their new sleeveless, lightweight frocks and bright-colored sandals. They also have altered their hair styles to validate the arrival of sweltering weather by shedding any encumbrance which hampers the flow of air.

Following that gusty announcement of the new season, the three snail-paced women enter in their traditional habits of dark, heavy and layered. Their somber disapproval of the new dresses is obvious. Combativeness over who is appropriately dressed gets this evening off to a rollicking start. Rivalry, competition and challenge are ignited assuring scopa to be lively. Everyday I have front and center seating to view the summer games and skirmishes from my balcony, now furnished with two bamboo chairs separated by a nice-sized weeping fig tree. Bridgie joins me today to be entertained by the antics below, while waiting for Gaines' arrival at seven-fifteen.

He changes into jeans, polo shirt and topsiders, joining me on the balcony for a chat before dinner.

"How was your day?"

"Oh, okay I guess. But I got upset at Riso."

"What happened?"

"First thing this morning when I got to the office, I received a memo from him stating that I owed the company over five milioni (about four thousand dollars) for the deposit on this apartment which was paid last October when we rented it and signed the contract."

"But you sent them the money the day after we returned to Illinois."

"Yes, and I showed him a copy of the receipt from my files. He is so disorganized that he doesn't know straight up. He also had the unmitigated gall to evaluate the price we're paying for this apartment and said that we should have negotiated for a lower price. How in the devil does he think we could negotiate anything when we could barely understand Fernanda or her attorney?"

"Well, they didn't provide us with an interpreter for that meeting or with an attorney for our protection either!"

"Another thing, if I hadn't been able to prove that I sent the deposit money, which he claims he has no record of, we'd have to pay him again. He never, ever has the correct information. Doesn't know enough to speak slowly to those of us who are trying to learn this difficult language." Gaines pauses thoughtfully while fingering the hair above his ear and reflecting on the events of his hectic day. "Your car came in today. They are checking it over. It will be delivered tomorrow evening."

I suddenly feel a little sick at that bit of news. I am privately scared silly to drive in Lecce, but I console myself with the thought that both Margie and Norma drive everywhere with Chet and Tom's cars. I guess I should accept the car if the company is willing to give me one, I reason, dreadfully.

"I'll practice driving during riposo while all those nutcases are napping. You know the only shift I've ever driven, Gaines, was on a steering column and *molti anni fa*" (many years ago.)

"You'll get used to it in no time at all. One of these days I'm going to Torino to a meeting, and you'll have to drive me to the airport."

"Tell me some good news," I say.

"Well, I love you very much. You're doing what a lot of women wouldn't."

"Wherever thou goest..."

He leans over to kiss me, at which time Bridget tries to pry us apart with her nose.

174

Gazing gargoyles of the human kind.

Gaines and I perceive that living in historic Lecce is multifaceted and a lot more frustrating than one could ever possibly imagine. There is no such thing as autonomy in our little corner of the world. The day we moved in we were tethered to the covey that devotes itself unselfishly to the affairs of those living within a certain range of notice. It is impossible to escape their meddlesome monitoring.

Not one member of the covey owns a car nor knows how to drive, but my new charcoal grey *Ipsilon Dieci* has the full attentiveness, contemplation and observation of i vicini. The hazardous, menacing, traffic accompanied with honking, shouts of damnation, and obscene gestures (plus having to familiarize oneself with the complicated, inconvenient layout of traffic patterns) is all taken in stride when driving in Italy. But the wearisome torment which awaits my arrival at home each day is sometimes more than I can endure.

As soon as I turn at the furniture refinishing shop, I see the gazing gargoyles, the Signorina and Gabriella at the end of the street, standing in their front French doors, keeping watch.

The tiresome procedure begins when I make the ninety-degree left turn. I acknowledge the onlookers with a smile, wave or friendly nod while adjusting the side mirror to enable a hair's breadth next to the house, endeavoring to park in a space between two doorways. The challenge of forward and reverse maneuvering, inching as near as possible to the stone house flush with the street, takes lots of practice especially when the Signorina stands in the street and shouts directions in the local dialect with her shrill ear-piercing voice, coupled with pounding on the front of the car, screeching, "Adriana, Adriana, Adriana," directing me to move a little bit forward or in the reverse. I apply the worthless blocca-sterzo, climb over the center console, exiting from the right side.

If that space is occupied, I park between Dominica's entrance and my own security gate. The Signorina hates this location, complaining that the morning sun reflects off the windshield into her front door, hampering her view. Sometimes she bullies Totó into draping a stiff, soiled canvas over the windshield and hood. She despises the presence of the car in that location so much that there are times when she uses the hood as a birdfeeder, sprinkling crusts of dried bread all over the new finish and attracting every feathered being in the area from the paunchy, nasty pigeons to the ubiquitous swallows.

The buzzer rings often and the message is always the same. "Adriana, move the car, a water truck or a moving van needs to get through." It is a continuous cry! After the first few weeks of this harassment, I rued the day I said, I would accept the vehicle.

Confronting savagery in the streets, at the Piazza, the post office, and the outdoor market, I have taken all the honing I can sustain for one morning and start home. Proceeding on a crowded, narrow, one-way street, a female driver behind me continues to badger me by pressing the horn all the way up the long incline. The flow of traffic is thwarted by children, shoppers, bikes and the elderly. I turn on the one-way lane at the Farmacia, slow to a necessary stop for a mother pushing a stroller in my path. Immediately the tormenting tail commences her ill-mannered annoyance. I coolly capture my taunter's reflection in the rear-view mirror, holding her gaze and turning off the ignition, I confine the mulish menace in place. The looking glass divulges an expression of helpless vexation, giving me much pleasure. It only takes sixty seconds to tame the shrew. I start the engine and drive home with the silenced chaperon in tandem. The tedious task of parking is accomplished, with the Signorina's assistance, and I enter the cortile feeling morose. Totó is seated shelling peas. "Now," he starts, "how would it be if this afternoon, likes, ya takes me out for a driving lesson?"

"Me? Teach you to drive? I can't do that! I can barely get around here myself!"

"Oh, come on! It will be easy, like."

"Tell me. Is it everyone's desire around here just to pester the life out of me?"

177

"*Stai tranquilla, signora.* (Be calm.) You'll be okay after you eats some of the purée. It turned out alright this morning."

"*Lasciami in pace*" (Leave me in peace), I say, climbing the stairs and yearning for a vacation to the States with garages, order, discipline, privacy, oh sweet privacy, no Eyetalians, and no "*ini*" spoken!

When Gaines returns from the office we chat on the balcony before dinner.

"Gaines, I simply will not let Totó involve me in his latest delusionary dream of me being his driving instructor. Talk about the blind leading the blind! Stefania told me that Totó has an English driver's license, but when he took the Italian test, he flunked it! It's curious to contemplate, no? I mean, how bad would you have to be, for heaven's sake, to flunk an Italian driving test?"

"Oh, he was fresh from England and probably didn't know who to pay off. I'll talk to him and maybe I can take him out to Chet's and let him drive around out there Saturday during riposo. By the way, tonight after our class, I have to take your car papers to the company's notary. His studio is near our new school."

28

The new Italian classes meet twice a week. The ladies are being taught by Signore Leone, who is about our age and speaks English well, with little accent. He is an American film buff and, no matter what the lesson is supposed to be, it always comes around to him leading a discussion on his favorite westerns! Signorina Antonietta Pucci is in her early thirties, and she is the instructor for the men. She has volunteered to accompany Gaines to the notary's studio after class. For a short distance they walk through a narrow street no wider than three meters, when suddenly in all of it's splendor the Basilica unexpectedly appears, glistening white from recent restoration.

"Oh!" Gaines gasps.

"It's construction was started in the 1620s and provided work for the local artisans for one-hundred-fifty years," offers Antonietta.

The architectural masterpiece is breathtakingly beautiful. Gaines gazes in amazement.

"Lecce Baroque is not emphatic nor pompous, but rather spontaneously elegant and ebullient. It is graceful and refined," Antonietta points out. They cross the street and continue a few meters. "*Eccoci qua!*" (Here we are!)

Notaio is impressively engraved on a brightly polished brass plate mounted on a beautiful wood paneled door. They go upstairs to an attractive receiving room with the customary vaulted ceiling.

A male secretary ushers them inside the stately office and Antonietta initiates the introductions. Gaines offers the notary the car documents with an inarticulate explanation. Ignored, he is given the cold shoulder, as the notary spouts *dialetto*.

Antonietta suggests. "If you will speak Italian slowly, this gentleman can understand you."

He ignores her suggestion and shows Gaines where to place his signature. The notary mocks him. *"Lui é mancino!"* (He is left-handed!) His laughter is scornful.

Gaines pays the fifty-thousand lire fee ($45), which the company will reimburse.

Leaving the office Gaines says, "I heard the remark he made about my being left-handed."

"Oh, it is a medieval prejudice and superstition. People who were left-handed were thought to be demon-possessed and villainous and sometimes, in certain regions, were killed. There are a lot of uneducated people here in the South who still consider it insulting. I heard two men talking about a woman. One said, 'Not only is she ugly, but she is left-handed!' I must say I'm not impressed with your company's notary. He is arrogant and boorish, which is uncommon for someone in his position. They have good educations and make lots of money here in Italy. If a person buys or sells property, the notary gets a percentage of the sale. My father says that it's a license to steal. His rudeness to you was certainly uncalled for."

"If he had spoken Italian slowly instead of the local dialect, I probably could have understood him."

"Are you joining the other Americans for dinner this evening?"

"No. Well, thanks for all your help. I must get home now." He feels badly about lying to her, but is confident Bobby will be grateful to him, because the young woman has chased Bobby ever since she found out his wife is in the States.

Gaines starts across the Piazza, stops at the edicola, and turns to watch her walk out of sight. He doubles back and joins me and the others at Guido e Figli Trattoria."

Margie, asks Gaines, while pouring him a glass of wine from a stainless steel pitcher. "How did you get rid of Antonietta?"

"I lied when she asked if I was going to meet you all for dinner."

Bobby exhales in relief. "I owe you one for that. Tuesday evening, as I left class, she tagged along beside me saying she wanted to see my new car. I showed it to her and then she asked if she could see the inside. I knew that if I unlocked it, she'd jump in and I'd never get rid of her. So I just pointed and said there it is, you can see it."

Chet raises his glass, "Let's have our toast."

"If we were all there, we wouldn't be here!" "Here, here," is said in unison.

Norma says, "I think I'm getting a bad reputation around town."

"Why?" I inquire.

"Well, I was trying to find cranberry juice the other day. I repeated the word given in my Eyetalian dictionary to several clerks in my area. My request was met with the strangest reaction. When I got home, I called Paola and told her of the incident and the word I was using. She laughed and told me the word I used means a poisonous berry. They probably think I'm trying to do away with Tom."

"I haven't seen cranberry juice anywhere. Have you, Margie?"

"No, but I'll bet we can get it up at the air force base. I'll check for you, Norma, when I go up to substitute for the fourth grade teacher next week."

"I did find those little plug-ins to kill the mosquitoes, though."

"Where?" Margie and I say in unison.

"At Superette. They are made by The Johnson Co., but I never saw that product at home."

"Margie, you're the lucky one this time," I remind her.

Norma laughs, "You have a dishwasher, Adrianne, I have a microwave, and Margie has screens!"

Margie changes the subject, "Tonight, Signore Leone drew a horrible looking face on the chalkboard with horns and

181

said, "*Diàvolo* (devil), my first wife!" If he isn't talking about American western movies, he draws stupid pictures. Is it too much to ask for us to have a good language teacher? First Whitecotton, who only wanted to insult us and now Leone, who tries to entertain!"

29

June is half over and it is getting hot. I am in and out of the car numerous times this morning running errands with Bridget, who loves to go in the car, sit in the front seat and sometimes hang her head out of the window.

"One last stop, Bridgie, and we'll go home." The main post office is situated in the middle of the daily open-air market. Finding a much coveted parking place is almost next to a miraculous happening, but I give it a try. After circling the block-long building thrice, I notice a shopper putting purchases in the trunk of a *Panda* and decide to wait for the car to exit.

I crack the windows for Bridgie and lock her inside. "Be a good girl, and I'll try not to be too long." The dog pushes her nose through the opening and wiggles her nostrils.

I enter the stately building and look for a window that is for parcel pickup. I observe the crowding around the windows. Just look at them, I think, they never form a line to them it is a gathering. How does one know who in the world to stand behind in this jamboree?

I take the card out of my purse and ask a lady to direct me to the right place. I am told to go into the next room. Observing the assemblage around the only window, I try to discern who is last in line. Standing on one foot and then the other, thoughts scatter from Bridget getting too hot in the car to thinking evil of anyone who sends a package thereby forcing me to endure this tedious exercise and having to pay the postage on it as well.

At long last I step up to the "huffish" clerk and hand her the card that had been sent by the post office informing me of a waiting parcel. The clerk reads it, looks at me suspiciously and asks for identification. I hand her the International and Illinois driver's license; both display recently taken photos. The postal employee has a superior, skeptical attitude which annoys me. She disappears with the IDs and returns a few moments later asking to see my passport, which is at home. This means that the same rigamarole will have to be played out tomorrow, because all of the Leccese are going to lock up in about ten minutes to go home for il pranzo and a long nap. The post office doesn't keep evening hours, as do most of the shops.

I become exasperated with the arrogant clerk. Revealing angered clumsiness I put the IDs in my bag, tear the postcard into little pieces and deliberately let them drizzle to the floor. In words the woman understands, I tell the clerk to go to the devil and take the parcel with her. I am vexed and vow they can keep the package, for I will never return.

I drive to Piazzetta Caduti sul Lavoro to Bar Euclide for lunch, I help Bridgie out of the car and select one of the outside tables that is in the shade. Securing the loop at the end of the leather lead under a chair leg, I sit down and try to gain some composure. I order a Coke and a rustico, telling the waiter to bring a cup of water for the dog. The anger and frustration is subsiding, and I am entertained by watching the bus boys using one arm to balance a tray with caffettiera, sugar bowl, demitasse cups and saucers, transporting it all by bicycle to nearby offices. They can finesse the traffic, people and animals. It is fascinating to watch them transport the piping hot beverage.

The comestible is placed on the small, round table with a Coca Cola served with a slice of lemon. I ask the waiter, "*Perfavore, vorrei del ghiàccio per* Coke." (Please, I would like ice for the Coke.)

"*Oh no, Signora. Il ghiàccio non va bene per i suoi polmoni.*" (Oh no, Mrs., ice is not good for your lungs). It is sincerely thought in Italy, that ice is not good for the lungs and I have met several people who hold to that idea.

"*Dimmi,*" I say, "*tu fumi?*" (you smoke?)

"Ah, sì, sì, sì, sì, sì,!"

184

"*Quante in al giorno?*" (How much in a day?)

"*Oh! Forse due pacchetti.*" (Maybe two packs.)

"*E stai dicendo che, il ghiàccio non va bene per i miei polmoni?*" (And you're saying ice is not good for my lungs.)   I laugh out loud and hand him the Coke.   "*Metti subito del ghiàccio in bevenda!*" (Put ice in this beverage, now!)   The absurdity of his viewpoint induces invigorating laughter, soothing my frayed nerves of the morning.

The waiter shrugs and gets my ice.

30

The morning sun cheers il nido and is already intense for the early hour.

"I miss having a morning paper delivered, "I say, and take another sip of my first cup of coffee.

"I miss having a pizza delivered, and in thirty minutes or less," Gaines adds.

"I miss grass and green foliage."

"I miss order and efficiency."

"I miss privacy," I groan, thinking of the covey.

"I miss not having hot water immediately for a shower."

"I've got a good one. I miss being able to use the dishwasher and oven simultaneously without tripping the circuit breaker."

"I miss having a garage of my own and an automatic door opener."

"I miss sidewalks."

"When we go home, we're going to buy a colonial-style house with a nice fenced-in yard for Bridgie."

"Oh, when we go home the Fourth of July and Thanksgiving aren't going to be the same this year."

"Well, I must get started." Gaines sets his cup and saucer on the trunk top. "Every morning, as I walk over to the garage, I dream of the last time I will have to do this. Oh, I intend to stop by the hospital this evening and visit Johnny Price. He was taken over there yesterday from work. He got very ill with phlebitis. I understand he's in pretty bad shape. He was to return to the States in a few days, but the doctor told him he won't be going anywhere for a while. Bobby went up to see him yesterday afternoon during his lunch break. Anyway, now get this, the patient has to provide their own towels for bath, cup and glass and utensils for meals, paper products tissues and toilet paper and their own bottled water for drinking." Gaines smiles, "But good ol' Johnny is so popular that his Italian friends are providing everything for him. He had twenty visitors yesterday. The hospital guard told Bobby he had never seen anything like it before and wanted to know who he is. Bobby also said that since there aren't any window screens and, of course, there's no air conditioning, the flies and mosquitoes are thick. Johnny made the mistake of killing a mosquito that left a bloody stain on his sheet, and now he will have to look at it for the next few days because bed linens are only changed once a week unless they are really soiled."

"That's a brand new hospital," I say.

"Bobby said they only use one bed pan and portable urinal for a whole ward of men and every time Johnny got it, he put it in his bedside table in an effort to keep it for his own use. There are women in the ward and no curtains. The sheet is your only privacy. The nurses came into dress a patient's leg which had been amputated recently. It was sickening."

"Gaines, when I think of how wonderful our hospital facilities are at home, it makes me so thankful to be born in the USA."

"We're fortunate and we ought to get down on our knees and thank God every day."

"Luciana was telling me that there is a movement now in the Italian Parliament called 'The Ticket' in English. What it means is some of the politicians want everyone to be responsible for paying a portion of the doctor's bill, the hospital bill and the medicine. She was livid. She said they already tax us to death for socialized medicine and it's still not enough. Well, anyway, the time is going fast and we have some lovely trips to look forward to while we're here."

Later the key turns in the front door, Totó rushes into the room. "Buon giorno signora. Briginella come stai?"

"Good morning, Totó."

187

The dog prances behind him with her tail up and swishing.

He opens the French door to the enclosed patio balancing the heavy crate of water bottles on his knee. Returning to the kitchen, he takes his cigarette in hand and says, "Have you noticed how fat Sofia has been gettin'?"

"Totó, I'm not going to discuss Sofia with you!"

Undaunted, he continues, "She eats like a bloody pig!"

"*Basta*" (Enough), I say, filling the dishwasher with the breakfast dishes and washing the coffee pot.

"I haven't slept with her in months!"

"*Basta cosi*! I'm leaving the house now. Bridgie is coming with me."

"Well, it's true, like."

"Who cares, it's nobody's business." I leave the kitchen.

The dog hangs her head out of the window, as we drive around the old Piazza down past the castle, taking a left through a narrow rabbit run lined with little boutiques. "This is our lucky day, Bridgie. A car is leaving in front of the Pasticceria Gelateria Prato, terrific!" I ease the *Ipsilon Dieci* into the vacated space close to the cement planters filled with palms. I lock the car doors leaving air cracks for Bridgie. "I'll be right back, Lovey. Be a good girl."

Remembering the lace shop down the street, I decide to make a quick trip to it before buying Gaines' favorite *stracciatella* (chocolate chip) ice cream at the Gelateria. My departure to buy the lace border for an altar cloth takes a few minutes. I am contented with my purchase and happily reflect on the design of the alternating chalice and cross on the lace edging. I approach the entrance of Prato's to find with horrific disbelief that the car is gone! I am stunned and visibly shaken. "I was only gone five minutes!" I say aloud. I scan the area and find that a parking attendant is checking cars a few meters from me.

"*Che é successo?*" *Dove sta la mia macchina?*" (What happened to my car?)

188

"Oh, signora. La macchina é stata portata al posto di polizia?" (Car was moved to the police station?)

"Perché?" (Why?)

"Lei non frequentata il bar." (You didn"t go into the bar.)

"Oh! É una trappola." (It is a trap.) *"Dove la stazione?"* (Where is the station?)

"Lei non lo sa?" (You don't know?)

"No!"

A loafer is listening to our conversation volunteers to take me to the parking lot of confiscated autos. I am so worried about Bridget that I get into the stranger's car and it isn't until he is driving out of the small Piazza that I realize I know nothing about him. How stupid, I think. I begin wondering how badly I would get hurt if I had to jump out of a moving vehicle. The man is true to his word and delivers me to the lot. I unlock the car and let the dog out taking her into the station with us.

The officer seated at a front desk is middle-aged and wears a black eye-patch. There is a name tag on his deep navy uniform identifying him as Officer Morelli. He is kind and asks the usual questions of what brings me to Lecce and for how long. I pay the fine and give the man who drove me there a tip and thank him graciously for his helpfulness. The officer walks me out to the car, helps the dog in and holds the door for me.

"Lei sta in casa domani?" (Will you be at home tomorrow?)

"Sì."

"Ci vediamo domani mattina alle dieci." (We will see each other tomorrow morning at ten.)

"Ma, mio marito non é in casa fino alle sette e mezzo nella sera. (But my husband is not at home until seven-thirty in the evening.)

As I drive away, I realize the significance of that last statement and how he may have mistakenly taken it. Why, I think, is he coming to see me anyway.

Scopa is shifted.

A chair placed in front of a second-hand store looks interesting. I stop. Its sturdy and certainly affordable. *"Puoi tagliare circa sei pollici dai piedi?"* (Can you cut about six inches from the legs?)

The dealer looks at me in disbelief. *"Come?"* (What?)

I repeat my request. The young man gives me a look of skepticism, thinking this American not only can't speak the language very well, but she must be strange, if she really means to shorten the legs. He forsakes any attempt to talk me out of it, promising to make the adjustment and deliver it after riposo.

I touch the lock release on the security gate for the dealer to make his delivery. The clicking sound echoes and can be heard to the back of the house. It is as useful as a red alert for "the one who has to know" that something is about happen. He prepares for his neighborhood watch and closely scrutinizes the second-hand dealer making his way through the cortile, carrying the new purchase by the arms, holding it above his head. I lead him into the living room and point to the open space between the fireplace and the antique chest. I toss a large cushion in the seat.

Stepping back, he smiles and says to me, *"Ah, sta comoda!"* (It is useful.) Noticing the telephone on the chest, he realizes my idea and gives me a look of approval putting to rest all questions of my rationality that he had earlier.

Behavior modification of i vicini has been stimulated by the lingering light of day and the penetrating rays of the sun. The ritualistic diversions of the after riposo activity is shifting its forum from the living room into the cortile. Gravitation is enthusiastically embraced, for it gives greater observation to the trafficking of others in the neighborhood. Curiosity of their comings and goings deem it necessary to gather up flat cushions used for makeshift tables, cards, refreshments and tobacco paraphernalia. They reposition themselves, sitting partially outside the opened security gate and scrunched into the eight-foot width of space of the porte-co-chere. To do this, they must first replace the blue scooter and the drying rack. Any

191

convenience can be sacrificed for the yearning to know all that happens on Via dei Sepolcri Messapici.

Gaines arrives at his usual time, disrupts the card game in order to enter, and shares greetings and laughter as he steps between the players. He looks up to see me and quattro zampe waiting on the balcony. After changing, Gaines joins us.

"How was your day?"

"Oh, typical, I guess. Scotti came down on the company plane for a meeting and returned to Torino this afternoon." Gaines fingers his sideburn reflecting on his day, displaying a smile.

"What?"

"Bobby was laughing about two of the Italians in the design department who had an argument today. One of the guys was convinced that the air conditioning works better with the windows open! Gee!" He shakes his head in disbelief. "What did you do today?"

"Outside of the fact that the car was towed away with Bridget in it, and that Officer Morelli, who is in charge of fines for towing, is going to call on me in the morning at ten, it was a normal day. And I bought a new chair."

"He what?"

"Well, I told him you wouldn't be home until seven-thirty!" I look at him laughing. "I naively assumed he would want to see you as well! Now I'm not so sure how he took it or what he wants, for that matter."

"Ha! He doesn't have any interest in seeing me. It's you he wants to get to know better, and I'm speaking of <u>know</u> in the biblical sense."

"Where are you going?"

"Down to have a little talk with Totó. This is a project he is suited for!"

31

Totó is busy sweeping in the dining room as I come down the stairs, fumbling in my bag for the car keys. Bridget's usual behavior is to run for the door when she hears the jingle of the metal, but this morning she sits down and puffs out one side of her upper lip, a perturbed expression she has used since puppyhood. It is obvious that she is in no hurry to get back into that car.

"Oh, Precious! Was yesterday's experience of being towed away in the car too much for you?" I pat her soft head and throat.

Totó, taking all this in, is provided with a perfect opening. "I understands from Gaines, like, that you're expecting a visitor this morning at ten o'clock." He giggles with relish.

"Totó, I do not need this kind of aggravation. Isn't the life over here difficult enough for us without this kind of a situation to top it off?"

"Don't worry! If I can't handle him, I'll turn Sofia on him. He'll be sorry he was ever born!"

This comment brings laughter to us reflecting on Sofia's celebrated tirades.

"I'm going to Norma's and then on to the big market."

"Enjoy yourself and try to stay out of trouble, like. Last time you went, you had your purse stolen."

"Ya, ya, ya."

I stop at a fabric store on my way to Norma's. I want another piece of green wool felt identical to one I purchased a few days ago for a desk top. I request the same bolt from the owner who waited on me previously. He measures, cuts, and writes out the cost on a slip of paper. I see that the amount for the exact same thing is more than before.

"*Signore, questa é piu cara.*" (This is more.)

"No."

"Sì."

"No, signora."

"*Io non pago questo.*" (I'm not paying this.) "*Ho pagato venticinque mila lire tre giorni fa. Io non pago trenta-due per la stessa cosa oggi.*" (I paid twenty-five thousand three days ago. I will not pay thirty-two thousand for the same thing today.)

He argues, makes excuses, and tries to hand me the felt.

"No." I push the material toward him on the counter and turn to leave the shop.

He gives in and changes the amount to *venticinque mila lire*. I hand the cashier the material and sales slip. The woman, who is the owner's wife, says with synchronized rhythm, punching the keys on the register. "Brava signora!"

I laugh. "Grazie molto, signora."

Returning to the house after Norma and I lunch at Raffaellos, I am met by Totó. "That bloke Morelli came by here about eleven o'clock, like. I didn't open the gate, but I asked him what he wanted. He said he wanted to talk to your husband." Totó rolls back his eyes in mockery. "I told him he wasn't in and he left."

"Thanks, Totó. I sure appreciate your help. What are you all having for lunch today? Smells good."

"*Spaghetti cornuti,*" he says, displaying the vulgar sign of cuckolding with his fingers.

"What's that?"

He gives his mischievous giggle and explains. "Oh, it is an old Italian name for spaghetti tossed in oil and garlic. It's fast and easy, you know, like the neighbor's wife, so to speak."

"You are unbelievable!"

32

A peaceful coexistence has lasted for about as long as everyone within the covey can stand, and Domenica has been getting on everyone's nerves lately. She is the likely candidate for a new conflict. Her dominance is a continual threat to Totó's need for leadership. Tensions have been mounting for some time, and now Totó has grown so weary of the constant prattle, the interruptions, and the influence she has with Sofia and Stefania. Domenica puts ideas of independence from his authority into their heads. He is looking for a way to rid her from the covey. With this weighty subject consuming his thoughts, he comes upstairs to work.

I am using an old, worn-out hand towel to swat the pesky mosquitoes. Their demise leaves fine-lined red streaks across the white walls, making a hideous design. I enjoy the extermination of the menacing stingers which create a whir, awakening us out of our slumber. An American friend from Torino, Burt Rossiter, has installed mosquito netting over each bed, but it can't be used effectively because of Bridgie's comings and goings during the night.

Carrying a broom, Totó joins me in the master bedroom. He stops, puts both hands on top of the handle and grins as he observes the red streaks that have materialized as a result of my atypical morning activity.

"Sofia will wash that off when she comes up. Every bedroom in Italia has the same decorations, like."

Sofia comes in carrying a cleaning bucket full of supplies. "You all right?"

"*Sì, non c'é male* Sofia. *Comé va?*" (Not bad, how are you?)

195

"Oh, così, così." (So, so.)

Displaying a mischievous twinkle in his eyes, Totó picks up the throw rugs and proclaims, "I'm going to get rid of that bloody Domenica today when she comes for caffé."

I turn in his direction and wrinkle my brow. "Where did that come from?"

"I'll put me hands on her big fat ass, and that will get rid of her nosy interfering ways."

"I don't know, Totó. You might be letting yourself in for more than you bargain for. She's been a lonely widow for a long time now and she might just love your advances. Then where would you be?" I wink at Sofia, who throws back her head laughing out loud.

The idea is so repugnant to Totó that he has to rethink his so-called strategy. Taking the rugs out on the balcony to shake out, he says, "I hate that bloody bitch. She farts so loud when she passes the gate, you'd think it was a bloody horse."

A while later I enter the kitchen, placing a pile of clothes on the table.

"What are you going to do with them clothes?"

"Oh, Totó, I need to discard these things. Do you have any ideas?"

"Sì. Stefania has friends that can wear them."

"Fine. They're welcome to them." I wonder who the clothes will show up on.

Sofia is cleaning out the refrigerator as she and Totó are conversing in the Leccese dialect when all of a sudden Totó strikes a nerve with her. She becomes so angry that her face flashes crimson, and she lays into him with such fury that I expect her to smack him up against the wall in the same fashion that the mosquitoes met their demise earlier. It's a good thing Sofia doesn't have a towel handy, I'm thinking.

After unleashing her venom, Sofia turns to me and says very sweetly, *"Ci vediamo stasera per caffè,* me darlin'." (We'll see each other this evening for caffè.) She leaves the house.

Totó moves one hand very fast in a chopping motion while blowing air from puffed up cheeks, demonstrating he'd like to cleave Sofia into little pieces.

I go into the guest room and see Giuliana rock her Cinquecento up the stone street. She escorts Daniela in for her English lesson, clucking to her chick through the cortile and up the stairs. Entering the house she pulls a handmade sweater from a bag and puts it up to my shoulders. *"É perfetto, bella no?"* (It is perfect and beautiful no?)

"Bella sì, Giuliana, *grazie molto."* (Beautiful, yes and thanks.)

"Ah, non fa niente." (It is nothing.) She turns to Daniela and clicks off numerous instructions.

The teenager responds, "Sì mamma, sì mamma, sì mamma, sì mamma." As soon as Giuliana leaves and Daniela sighs with relief. "Mamma mia!"

"Dani, your mother designs and makes beautiful knitwear. Does she have a knitting machine?"

"Yes. She loves to do that."

The lesson goes well and Dani's father picks her up at five-forty-five.

This evening we eat at Rollo's and afterwards enjoy a stroll to the Piazza. When we return home we are met by Domenica, coming from Totó's front room. She hastens toward us with a serious expression as we enter the gate. Oh dear, I remember his threats early this morning.

"Un cugino di Sofia *é morto oggi."* (A cousin of Sofia's died today.)

We enter Sofia's dimly lit front room with Domenica. I notice my discarded flowered designer T-shirt pulled over Sofia's body like sausage casing. We hug her and express our sympathy, which she accepts, weeping profusely.

Domenica helps her sit down on the settee saying, "*coraggio, coraggio,* Sofia." (Courage.)

Sofia still clinging to Gaines' hand pulls him down next to her. Unfortunately her well set tourniquet grip has locked all circulation, and his hand is throbbing. Everyone in the covey is present except Totó, who is coming in now with his attention glued to an inside page of his newspaper. He takes reading glasses from his breast pocket saying, "Stefania, turn on the lights in this bloody morgue. I can't see a thing to know how to fill out the scores, like."

Stefania obeys his wishes and Sofia lets out another loud bellow, mopping her face and eyes with a handkerchief. The three septuagenarians, Domenica and Tiziana say in unison, "Coraggio, coraggio cara."

Totó looks over his paper and asks, "Now, Gaines, does ya think Lecce, even though we're in Series A, can beat Napoli like, in Sunday's match?"

Gaines still remains restricted and is hesitant to respond to Totó's insensitive question, giving him a shrug.

"I think I'll go with Juventus like, over Milano."

Sofia's sobs are followed again by a chorus of coraggio.

We don't dare look at each other for fear of succumbing to hysterics. More friends and family enter the room enabling us to leave, followed by Totó who carries his soccer form out into the cortile.

"Was Sofia close to her cousin?" I ask.

"Hell no! He lived in Naples. She only saw him a few times in her life. You see, it's like this. Sofia loves the drama and getting herself all worked up, like. Just you watch. Tomorrow she'll be dressed up in black and wear it God only knows how long. She loves the attention, like. It gives her something to do."

*

It is Friday evening and Gaines is trying to drive up overcrowded Libertini on his way home, grateful that another

198

week is over. He is looking forward to the weekend and dinner tonight at La Luna nel Pozzo (The Moon in the Well) with the Americans. He unlocks and lifts the steel shuttered security door of the garage and drives into the vacant dimly lit cavern. Proceeding cautiously through the first two rooms, making a sharp right turn, he drives to the far end of the third and last vaulted, ceilinged chamber to his assigned parking place. The object now is to hightail it to the entrance before the automatically timed lights go off.

As he steps out of the car, a clamorous sound startles him so that he is immediately stricken with weakening fear, and the juice is drained right out of him. The spooky outburst is coming from a window nearly fourteen feet above. Endeavoring to make a quick getaway from the unknown menace, he hears a voice, "signore, signore."

Grazie Dio, he thinks. It's the cleaning lady. He looks up and sees her clearing the collected debris from the inset of the window pane. Her broom had incited his nightmarish panic. She is a funny, little knotted-up person who is at Signora Quarta's side unceasingly.

Valerio has given up his car washing and oil changing business for a new career of making sandwiches. So the Signora and her sidekick cleaning lady, referred to as Sancho Panza by Gaines, are operating the garage by themselves and have it cleaned up and organized.

Gaines' speedy exit from the darkened tomb is hampered by lessened leg strength from fright, but he manages and in a short time, finds himself turning the key in the front gate. Stefania comes up behind him. She is all smiles, carrying a large box wrapped with the dress shop's name and address artistically designed on the paper. It is tied with a narrow, ribbed ribbon which has been curled with the opened edge of scissors.

"Hi, Stefania. How are you?"

"Great. I just bought a new dress for Tiziana's wedding."

They wave to me and Bridgie on the balcony. Totó is wearing glasses and seated near the stairway. He moistens the end of his pencil and proceeds to mark his soccer picks for the lottery. "Do you think Torino will beat Napoli, Gaines?" Not waiting for an answer nor looking up, Totó says, "I'm goin' with Torino. I can't stand that bloody Maradona, the stupid show off! They ought to send him back to Argentina where he belongs."

"Sounds good to me, Totó."

"Do you want to see my new dress?" Stefania asks me.

"Sure."

The excited girl unwraps the box. Shaking out a black, tailored-looking garment, she holds it up by the shoulders for me to see.

"Very smart."

Totó does not bother to look at the dress he has paid for and keeping eyes solely on the scores, asks sarcastically, "Who died?"

"It's ready when you decide!" she retorts.

We don't try to stifle our laughter.

*

The next day Gaines and I are discussing an invitation I've received.

"You mean she invited us to come at nine in the evening? That's only an hour before we go to bed!"

"Oh, well Gaines, it's Saturday night, and church doesn't start until ten-thirty. Let's go and enjoy ourselves."

"Well, did she mean for dinner or what?"

"Flavia didn't explain a thing. She saw me coming across the Piazza. She stopped her car, jumped out, gave me a cheek to cheek and says, ' I'm having a party Saturday night. Come at nine.' Besides, Gaines, you've got to see the house! It is like no place you've ever been before. It's something straight out of the movies."

I remember back to last June, when Beatrice Strada had escorted five of us Americans, who were seriously interested in the relocation, on a short walk from the Risorgimento Hotel through the confusing maze of Baroque, and into the past.

200

When we arrived at the Palazzo on Via Marco Basseo, it impressed all of us.

Flavia's father has an Oriental rug business on the ground level. We browsed in his elegant shop before going up to the living quarters. Outside the shop we entered the huge, oval-topped carriage doors, which lead into a sizeable parking area of the porte-co-chere.

The triple staircase is to the left and a marble railing is supported by a series of balusters. The staircase takes a ninety-degree turn at a landing to *primo piano* (first floor, second floor to Americans.) I recall the magnificent paneled door with an engraved brass name plate.

A maid answered the door and escorted us into a huge drawing room, about eight-hundred square feet, where we were received by Flavia. Her black hair was pulled straight back into a chignon and fastened with a black plastic hair ornament. Flavia's exotic appearance betrayed the Turkish blood of her father, as well as the Greek of her mother, who was having a party of her own at a card table at one end of the huge salon.

We were introduced and seated. I reminisce about the handpainted scenes framed in plaster moldings on the ceiling. A sparkling, multifaceted, crystal chandelier hung from the center.

The maid brought in a bottle of well-chilled Asti Spumante Brut. Flavia's very attractive, blonde-headed mother proposed a toast to us. She and her friends were well-dressed, coifed, and bejeweled sixtyish grand dames.

I commented to Norma, who was seated next to me on the Louis XIV settee, "Will that be us in twenty years?" We laughed together, not knowing what the future held.

"Well, I guess we better go, but I think I'll eat a snack anyway," Gaines says, looking into the refrigerator. "Where did you get that tape?"

"At the market. Do you like it?"

"Yes, who is it?"

"His name is Al Bano. Antonietta told me he is married to Tyrone Power and Linda Christian's daughter, Romina. She

201

sings with him as well. Evidently they made films together when they were young. They have been married for years and have several children."

"I like his sound."

"I do, too. We should get our group together and go up to his restaurant. He has a home there surrounded by grape vineyards. I understand he has apartments and some of the Americans from San Vito Air Force Base live at what they call Power Estates."

"What is the name of that song?" Gaines takes me in his arms, and we dance around the table in the kitchen.

" *'Pensando a Te,'* Thinking of You."

The next song on the tape begins. The name of it is *La Canzone di Maria* (The Song of Maria.) It is very upbeat and Bridget gets into the spirit of the moment by prancing around the table with her tail up and swishing almost keeping time with the music, amusing us.

We intentionally arrive at Flavia's door thirty minutes late, and to our surprise we are the first guests but it isn't long before the other guests come in, filling the salon with multilingual conversation.

A buffet of international cuisine is set out at eleven-thirty. Flavia's father has prepared some Turkish specialties. Maria, Flavia's mother, serves Greek dishes, and of course Italian food is present.

As we walk home Gaines says, "I met some interesting people tonight."

"I'm glad. It was nice of Flavia to invite us. She is a good hostess."

chiesa del Gesù

Part III
Nothing Will Ever Be The Same Again

33

The plant goes on holiday for the month of August, as does most of Italy. Italians either go to the mountains or to the sea. We returned to the States except for Bridgie, who remained in Lecce with Totó, Sofia, and Stefania. Gaines paid Totó one-hundred thousand lire (about $90) for his trouble.

On our way back to Lecce, we come through New York and when we get to Alitalia terminal at Kennedy Airport, it looks and sounds like little Italy!

"Sounds like our people," remarks Gaines.

When he said that, something inside of me caused my spirits to soar, and I realize I am anxious to return to our new life and start meeting the challenges that are in store for us.

We go up to the lounge for business-and first-class passengers. The television is turned to Rai Uno and a familiar female newscaster is giving the pre-recorded evening news from Rome. We take espresso, pick up today's Italian newspapers and sit down near some Italians. It is difficult not to eavesdrop on their conversation and stare at their gold jewelry, designer clothes, and leather goods. Upper-class Italian women exude a casual elegance with impeccable style.

I realize our new life can't be shared with or understood by the friends and family left in the States, and even some of the American colleagues in Lecce who are not embracing the life with as much fervor as we. The enthusiasm felt for our new life is cultivating a change in us, and I recognize now that nothing will ever be the same again.

A week later Gaines has just returned with Briginella from their morning outing. I am dressed and ready for church. I carry the coffee tray downstairs and the phone rings. We look at each other wondering if it is a call from the States as it would be in the wee hours of the morning there. Gaines answers, "Pronto." I catch a glimpse of his sober expression. "I'm sorry to hear that."

I quietly carry the tray into the kitchen trying to hear what he is saying.

Putting the receiver down, he says, "That was Tom. He and Norma went down to their garage this morning. When he unlocked the box, there was no car, just an empty space. Someone managed to get through the security gate and the locked box.

"We should be with them. Let's take them to the Questura. We certainly know how they feel. I thought if anyone's car was safe, it was theirs. How could the thief get through two locks?"

"Tom said that he suspects an inside job. You phone them and tell them we'll be over to pick them up in fifteen minutes, and I'll get my keys and documenti."

"First their house is burglarized, and now this. Norma doesn't like it over here anyway. It is so discouraging. Oh, hi Tom, Gaines and I will be over to take you all to the Questura."

"What for?" Tom asks.

"Oh, for whatever help we can be. See you soon, goodbye."

"Bridgie, you be a good girl," Gaines says, pointing at her. She walks to the front door and waits for us to open it. As soon as it opens, she is out of here and downstairs slapping Totó's door, which gives way. Bridgie prances into the front room, receiving their love and approval.

Sofia and Totó come out to greet us all smiles, and we just about double up with laughter because Totó is wearing Sofia's new black flowered dress for fall. It is obvious he has been enlisted to help Sofia put in a new hem because part of the bottom edge has been pinned, but Totó, always the clown, sashays out into the cortile. He is bare legged, clumping along in his Dr. Scholl's sandals. Turning slowly, putting his hand up to his face, he bats his eyes and comes back to the front entrance as if he is on the cat walk in Milano.

"Bravo," I applaud. "You'll probably receive offers from Milano soon."

"I couldn't possibly leave my cleaning job on Friday morning!"

"You all right?" Sofia inquires.

"We are a little upset, Sofia. Norma and Tom's car was stolen last night, and we're going over to take them to the Questura."

"Oh, Madonna!" she exclaims. "Jesus, Mary and Joseph!"

"We'll all be back here for lunch after church as planned. The tables are set and everything is ready to go."

"We'll bring up the *Parmigiana di melanzane* (baked eggplant in sauce and cheese) for lunch, about one-thirty, after everyone arrives."

"Oh, I can't wait, Sofia," Gaines says.

After Tom fills out the necessary forms and the report has been completed, Gaines suggests, "Do you feel like going to church with us, or would you rather go to the Duomo Bar for caffé?"

"We'd like to go to your church," Tom says. "Wouldn't we, Norma?"

"Oh, yes. This may be the only opportunity we'll have since we've decided to attend services up at the base."

"I warn you it's all in Italian, but the hymns are familiar," I add.

"It will be fine," answers Norma.

"The congregation is small and very friendly. Everyone of them will kiss you on each cheek hello and goodbye!"

"Really?" Tom asks.

"*Anche gli uomini*" (Also the men), Gaines laughs.

Ginny Rae Taylor, a sixtyish American lady, who thirty-six years ago founded the church with her recently deceased husband, greets us at the door. She possesses a gracious, refined manner.

"Pino, Tom and Norma had their car stolen out of their box in the basement garage of their apartment building sometime between nine-thirty last evening and six this morning," offers Gaines.

"Oh, I'm so sorry. We'll pray for you and the return of your car this morning," responds the pastor.

Sergio Gallo is in the small group of parishioners listening. He is fluent in English because of time spent in England when he was a child. He becomes quite curious about the theft and volunteers to inquire around. "I might be able to find out something for you of the car's whereabouts."

Gaines' curiosity is peaked as to his sincerity in this area and thinks he's showing off. After all, he is a shop owner, not a policeman or detective.

Tom says, "Thank you very much. I would appreciate anything you might be able to do."

"Where do you live, Tom?" Sergio inquires. Tom gives Sergio his address.

"What is the make, model, and color of your car?"

Gaines wonders what Sergio can possibly do. He's carrying on like an investigator in charge and gives Tom a puzzled expression with raised eyebrows.

That evening after the departure of the Americans and the last dish is put away, I drop to the sofa in il nido, kick off my shoes and put my feet on the wooden, flat-topped trunk.

The phone rings. "Maybe that's Pierce," I call down to Gaines, who picks up the receiver. He isn't calling me down to talk, so it must be someone else. Shifting a little, I squeeze a small firm cushion into the hollow of my back.

Gaines slowly and thoughtfully climbs the stairs. By his expression, I know he is concerned.

"Well, who was it?"

He looks me in the face with total disbelief. "That was Tom. Soon after Chet and Margie took them home, they received a telephone call from the thief. It seems he is holding the car for ransom. He asked for lire, about the equivalent of fifteen-hundred dollars for the return of the car."

"They're holding it for ransom?"

"Yes. Tom told him, 'No way. You can keep the darn thing. I won't pay it.' "

"Well, good for him. Besides, the company will give him another car tomorrow."

The parishioners at the Christian Church of Lecce never take very seriously the time a meeting is supposed to start. The pastor, Pino Neglia, is well aware of his people's ways. He knows it is useless to get upset or to try to change them about their tardiness.

"By the way Gaines, I'm telling you and Adrianne that the morning service is now officially at ten forty-five instead of ten-thirty. I'm not informing the others because in time they will push it to eleven and then it will be eleven-fifteen. You and Adrianne and a few others are the only ones who show up on time. I've talked until I'm blue in the face, and they promise me that they'll change and be punctual. Hmm." Pino shrugs and gestures with his right hand. "It lasts one, two, maybe three weeks, and then they slip back into their old ways."

However, we notice that there is one activity that is held on time that peaks everyone's interest, men as well as women: the Agape potluck dinner is given on every fourth or fifth Sunday after the morning service. When the final song and prayer of dismissal is given, each lady makes a mad dash home to take piping hot dishes out of the oven, returning to the church building through much traffic. As they enter the church, they find it has been transformed into a dining hall by some of the men and older boys.

Anyone can take part in the planning, but only certain ones are asked to prepare the first plate, which is a pasta, potato or rice dish. This plate is considered the most important of the many courses that are served. Ginny Rae organizes the serving. She found early in her experience that it is best for everyone to

207

be seated and to have a small group of the ladies serve each course because Italians don't queue up!

I play it safe and volunteer to bring a large salad, as well a large braid of mozzarella fresca, which is served before dessert with a drizzle of extra virgin olive oil, salt and pepper.

Gaines and Pino are seated next to one another during the meal.

"Gaines, did Tom ever get his car back?"

"The thief asked him for a ransom."

"That is done a lot here, Gaines."

"Tom of course refused. The company provided him with another car the next day. Sergio certainly acted interested in Tom's car. He even told Tom he might be able to recover it for him. That really surprised me. He's a shop owner, isn't he?"

Pino throws his head back and shakes it exhaling with a pained expression. "Ah, si. Sergio knows a lot of sordid stuff. He comes from a Mafia family."

"Is he a Christian?" Gaines asks.

"Ah, he is baptized, but! The whole family is deeply rooted in the mafia. The business he inherited from his father is financially indebted to the organization. It is a real problem. One of his relatives is a big boss! Several of the men in the church want to help get him another start. We donate food to help him and his family. *É una brutta situazione!*" (It is an ugly situation!)

34

The month of September is almost over and the time has come to take Bridgie to the veterinarian for rabies vaccination. This is not required in Puglia, but to re-enter the States her shots have to be continued each year. Dr. Vito Molle has been recommended by Luciana. He has cared for all of her domestic animals for many years and had been a friend of her mother. The animal clinic is off an alleyway behind the Duomo.

I park in an undesignated space in an overcrowded smallish lot in front of the clinic. We enter the vet's surgery on the ground floor. It is full of dogs and cats of diverse breeds. The owners manifest identical expressions of grim, long-faced boredom.

At long last it is our turn to go into the only examining room which is attended by four veterinarians donned in the official long, white, heavily starched coats. The seasoned Molle, his daughter and two unidentified gentlemen vets hoist the nervous and shaking setter onto the examining table positioned in the center of the room under a very bright light.

Each doctor takes a preassigned area on her quaking body. One lifts her tail and inserts a thermometer. Another shines a light into her eyes, mouth and ears. Dottoressa Molle listens to the heartbeat while her father feels Bridgie's tummy and moves her joints and limbs.

The exam comes to a synchronized pause. The staff converses with the senior member. They nod in agreement on the soundness of her condition, and Dr. Molle writes out the prescription for the rabies vaccine and directs me to the nearest pharmacy.

I lead the dog to the car, lock her inside, proceed down the alley, turn the corner and see the pharmacy just ahead. I am muttering to myself, "Nothing is easy, efficient or convenient in Italy! The only thing they do with efficiency is bury! If a person dies one day, the funeral service and burial is the very next day. I've been told it is because they don't embalm the body. As a result of this hurried activity, black posters are pasted to the stone houses and walls of the city announcing the death of the person because there isn't time to put it in the *Quotidiano*." (Daily News.)

My mission is accomplished and I dislodge the puzzled-looking canine from her temporary confines and attempt to re-enter the clinic with a big protest on the other end of the leather lead. "Look, Briginella. I don't think much of their methods either, but we have no choice but to go back in there so you can get your injection."

She sets her paws with so much resistance that I can hardly budge her. Finally we are inside the waiting room once again and marking time until it comes around to our turn. The vaccination is given and the tedious ordeal is over.

Stepping from the asphyxiating, disinfecting odor into the fresh, warm air, Bridget and I feel the relief of having completed the necessary mission. My eyes grasp the familiar inlet of space just off the alleyway about thirty meters from the clinic entrance.

"Oh, let's go over and see the cats." Bridget responds by giving her sienna plume a boost coupled with a light-spirited gate. We reach the tall, black wrought iron restraint as we look through the alternating, spaced metal doweling. "I count seven cats already." Surveying the small unearthed First Century Roman Amphitheater, I notice that it has become a haven for homeless felines.

Bridget and I have stood here on other daily outings, traipsing around the old city on expeditions, discovering Lecce's past, which is visibly substantiated by the physical remains both above and below the earth's surface.

Evidence includes pre-Christian, Greco-Messapician people lying in their burial chambers, which have been discovered in recent years. The chambers reveal ornamental marble friezes and carved stone inscriptions in a language not yet deciphered.

The Romans bequeathed two amphitheaters between 97 and 117 A.D. during the reign of Trojan.

A cemetery is thirteenth-century Romanesque near the half-Byzantine, half-Moorish abbey and church dedicated to Saints Niccolò and Cataldo was founded in 1180 (according to the stone set into the cloisters) by Tancredi, Count of Lecce.

The castle, a sixteenth century fortress surrounded by a moat at one time, was ordered to be built by Carlo Quinto (Charles V). Its design and construction was done by the military architect Gian Giacomo dell'Acaya from Lecce. And, of course, there is the awesome Leccese Baroque of the seventeenth century, plus a column which marked the Appian Way, now standing in the old Piazza. Everytime we pass a valley south of Lecce on the way to Otranto, I think of Homer. I was told by an American colleague that he wrote *The Odyssey*, there when he was on his way home from the fall of Troy; however, I have not found it documented.

So many people from other parts have invested time and talent here in this remote region of Italy. I contemplate the brevity of time one has and wonder how many life experiences have influenced, touched, given, labored, settled, breathed the air and soaked up the same sun's rays as I am this morning in moments of reflection. The four midwesterners are designing and directing an engineering department, overseeing the building of a new laboratory, and testing the equipment. I wonder if their contribution will leave a mark, a trace of light for future folk to discover and study. We are only a snippet of a remnant but my goodness, what a tremendous patchwork we have become a part of, two thousand years of extraordinary accomplishments right here in Lecce, from chariots to construction machinery.

211

35

"What's on for today, Adrianne?" Gaines asks, as he takes another sip of coffee.

"I asked Norma to bring her sister and cousins over for lunch. They'll be leaving on their European tour tomorrow, and we won't have another opportunity to see them."

"You better go to the bank. We'll need extra cash for the holiday coming up. I don't work Monday because it's *tutti i Santi,* All Saints Day."

"Well, I hope they aren't on strike today. That has happened several times in recent months. I never before heard of bank employees striking or school kids, for that matter! They need their bottoms wacked."

"Who? The bank employees or the kids?"

"Both!"

"I never realized how much I took for granted at home. You can always count on the bank being open, unless it is a holiday."

It is mid-morning and I drive to Piazza Mazzini and find a space open on the square and park between the marked diagonal lines near the bank. No strike, no lines and the computers are working. How did I get so lucky this morning, I think, as I leave the bank with my spirits lifted. I pay the parking attendant and prepare to back out of the space. He is directing traffic on the one-way street behind me and motions for me to exit. I cut the wheel a little to the right, carefully easing out of the space when I feel a crunch on my back bumper. Turning around I see a brand new, shiny red Fiat Uno. The driver notices me leaving and misjudges the timing in hopes of parking in my place. He irresponsibly gambles on beating me and tries to back past me before I can back out of the space.

"Ohhh, what an idiot!" I loosen my seat belt. "At least I have the attendant as a witness," I say to myself.

The driver of the Uno jumps out and begins crying around about his dented door. His animated gestures of pointing to the unsightly car and hitting his head dramatically brings no sympathy from me.

"*Ha sbagliato!*" (Your mistake!) I say to him, as I examine my car and see only a streak of faint red paint which easily wipes off the black plastic bumper with a tissue.

We exchange the normal information. "Eyetalians!" I yell, and drive a few blocks to the Snack Bar. There I purchase prepared foods from the steam table for my luncheon guests, taking care to choose foods characteristic of the Puglia region.

The first plate will be *Orecchiette con le Rape,* which are small thumb-sized dumplings tossed with a green vegetable much like broccoli in light olive oil, a hint of anchovy, a little red pepper and salt. I select *Pollo arrosto* (roasted chicken) seasoned in aromatic herbs (kitchen sea salt, rosemary, basil, garlic, juniper, and sage). Fresh fruit, Mozzarella fresca, and Gelato are also purchased. One of the waiters helps me carry the food to the car.

It is one of those glorious end-of-October days. The atmosphere seems to be electrified by some unknown source. Halloween isn't observed here but November 1, All Saint's Day, is a holiday for memorial observance. It is a time to visit the cemetery and decorate the tombs. The flower stands are in abundance everywhere. Huge mums, sheaves of gladioli, small cushion chrysanthemums, carnations and roses are on display.

Norma and her relatives decide to bring me a bouquet of the giant, white and yellow mums which are reminiscent of football games and autumn homecomings. Two activities that we long for here in the land of soccer! The proprietor of the flower shop is astute enough to know that these foreign ladies aren't buying for the deceased.

213

"*Un regalo?*" (A gift?)

"*Si.*"

"*Chi é?*" (Who is it?)

Norma nonchalantly smiles and says, "*Un' amica.*" (A friend.)

The shop owner looks horrified. "Signora no!" His spouse is arranging a bouquet and overhears the reply. She clucks her tongue, shakes her dark, ringlet covered head and rolls back her eyes asking, "*É un'amica Italiana?*"

"*No, Signora é Americana.*"

"*Che il nome?*"

"Adrianne Grant."

"*Dové abita?*" (Where does she live?)

"*A Lecce.*"

"*Va bene Signora, ma non regali mai questi fiori a un Italiana perché sono per il cimitero.* (Good, Mrs., but never a gift of these flowers to an Italian because they are for the cemetery.)

Norma relates the flower etiquette to her sister and cousins. "The shopkeeper said, 'chrysanthemums and carnations are used only to decorate the churches, tombs and pictures of the Madonna and Christ and should never be taken inside of the home. Evil spirits will then invade the house and bring bad luck.' His wife added, 'Never give a friend yellow roses, because it signifies envy.'"

The women laugh about the strange customs as they arrive at my security gate. They are chatty, full of enthusiasm and somewhat enchanted with the quaintness and charm of the historic district. As they enter the gate, Sofia is stooped over the rubber tree plant putting some nutrient into the soil. She casually looks up as the ladies walk toward her. Recognizing Norma, she smiles, notices the bouquet, which is properly carried upside down, to keep the water inside the stems. Her sight catches the huge white and yellow balls bobbing their heads next to the yellow, fluted-edged crepe paper. Sofia's cheerful expression plummets. Crossing herself she says, "Jesus, Mary and Joseph," hastens inside and shuts her door firmly.

I wait for the ladies on the landing, take the bouquet, and give them a cheek to cheek greeting. I just happen to glance down at my neighbor's door and notice the inside shutters are tightly closed. "You all have scared the wits out of poor Sofia. She'll probably have Father Caesare over here after riposo to perform an exorcism on my house! Haven't you been told that mums bring the evil spirits in with them, hum?" I put the lovely bouquet in the tall, blue vase. "These mums make me think of crisp autumn days, hayrack rides and apple cider."

"Oh, I miss this time of the year at home when the leaves turn, eating caramel apples and popcorn," says Norma.

"Italians don't eat corn the way we do. Gaines told me they consider it feed for livestock."

The telephone rings. "Pronto. Oh, hi, Margie! Can you come over and join us? Oh, no! When did it happen? Is there anything I can do? Well, goodbye then. I'll call you later."

"What's wrong?" Norma asks.

"Someone stole Margie's car right out of the Standa parking lot. She came out with all of her groceries and no car. Chet is there with her."

"Three of us down and one more to go. Bobby is the only one that is unscathed so far," remarks Norma.

*

It is a warm, sunny November 1, and Gaines drives, Totó, Sofia, Stefania and I to a nearby community to visit the cemetery where Totó's relatives are buried. The deceased are entombed in drawers, either in huge community mausoleums or in dwarfish sized, privately owned stone structures.

The decorative iron gates are opened, welcoming visitation inside the smallish rooms. Each private mausoleum has an altar with a white cloth edged in lace depicting designs of religious motifs. Bouquets and numerous lighted candles cast solemnity. Statues of the Madonna, Christ and pictures of the deceased are displayed.

Processions of family, friends and loved ones call on those of the past. We stand in front of the huge wall housing a myriad of drawers. Mounted frames for photos and attached miniature wall vases for a few flowers are individually provided for remembrance of the deceased interred.

Totó points to the yellowing photograph of his father and touches the drawer. He says, "I came out here the other day on me scooter, like, to see if I could move him to a smaller drawer. He's been here for fifteen years, you know, since he died, but we couldn't move him. He isn't ready because his legs wouldn't break, so we have to leave him here for another two years, like. He ought to be ready by then. The smaller boxes is cheaper. Besides they needs the larger ones for the new bodies."

He looks at Gaines and me. Listening, we are astounded by Italian customs. Totó continues, "His hair has turned all orange, like, and most of his face is gone now."

"How horrible for you to see him like that." I say, sympathizing.

"Well, it isn't pleasant, like, but somebody has to do it, and I didn't want my sister, Angelina, to see him like that. She couldn't have stood it."

As we ride back to Lecce, each one of us is entrapped in our own thoughts. We gaze out at the countryside. Gaines breaks the silence, "Hey, Totó, did we just pass a German pillbox from World War II?"

"Si. Not very far from here, when I was just a kid, I happened onto a German pilot who had landed in a field back there. I watched him get back into the plane and I thought I'd watch him take off, like, but when he started the engine, it caught fire and he couldn't get the top open, like. I felt so bad 'cause I couldn't help him. I stood there and, and . . ." Totó's voice cracks, "watched him. I just couldn't help him. I was helpless, like. I just watched him burn up."

216

Totó's memory still brings pain to him when he recalls it. We feel sorry for Totó, and a silence falls as we uncomfortably look out at the passing landscape of shepherd's huts, picked vineyards, and the rust-colored soil surrounding ancient gnarled olive trees. Each one of us is trying to think of something appropriate to say to him to ease his pent-up guilt and anguish.

36

Isabella Carlucci is a friend of Sofia's and somewhat older, in her mid-sixties. She is a widow and lives alone in her lifelong home, which is down the street, on the corner across from the furniture shop. She has one child, a son, who is married with children. He owns a restaurant at San Cataldo on the beach and has little time to pay attention to his mother or his aunt, Isabella's sister, who lives two doors from her. She is not company to Isabella, as the poor old soul has lost her mind and sits in her doorway all day long yelling '*puttana*' (whore) at everyone who passes, including some of the priests who live nearby.

I drive home from morning errands and shopping, when I notice Isabella standing in front of her house as if she is waiting for someone. I realize that Isabella was standing there two hours earlier. Surely she hasn't been there all that time. It's too cold to stand out there; even with her wraps on she looks frozen to the bone.

After riposo, Bridgie and I have been invited to caffé time before cards, which has been moved into Totó's front room for the fall and winter games.

Already present, the covey is huddled in their layers of woolens, and Totó is adding a shot of *Strega* liqueur to everyone's caffé. "Have a little of the witch. It'll warm you up, like," Totó says to me, as we arrive.

"Witch?"

"Ya, strega is Italian for witch."

After tasting it, I cautiously ask, "High in alcohol content, no?"

"Forty percent," he chuckles.

"What's with Isabella? I saw her this morning when I left for shopping then again when I returned two hours later."

"Oh, she has a ghost inside of her house and is afraid to go inside," mocks Sofia, laughing.

"Well, Mom, Isabella says the ghost tells her to stay out of the house and to not come in." Stefania rolls her eyes.

"She has a ghost who talks to her?" I ask, smiling.

"If you ask me, she's going crazy just like her sister," says Totó.

"Oh, Toe! You never liked her."

"Well, Sofia, if she's such a great friend of yours, you should go down there and spend the night with her tonight. I would be glad to go down there but it wouldn't look so good, like," giving his mischievous giggle. Sofia feigns a darksome frown in his direction.

When the cold weather comes, Totó doesn't have fishing, snails, or enough activity to stretch his energies. His otherwise playful disposition turns to tasteless and tactless needling of Sofia's and Stefania's overweight figures. It has become a preoccupation with him. He detests the way they have let themselves go. All of his teasing remarks, pleading, talking, and humiliation has been completely ignored, frustrating and infuriating him to no end. The crowded room is always his forum. Leaning over to me, he announces in a loud voice to be heard by all. "I'm livin' with two sacks of potatoes."

"Totó, if your intent is to motivate them into losing weight, you are going about it in the wrong way," I tell him.

The next morning the alarm sounds at six. I slip into a heavy robe and furry house slippers to avoid stepping barefoot, especially first thing in the morning, onto the inhospitable chilly marble floor. Gaines hurriedly gets into his running suit, shoes, and pullover sweatshirt, shakes a very drowsy dog and out they go for a short jaunt.

I mechanically move down to the kitchen, put water on for Bridgie's four-minute egg and break melba toast into a stainless steel bowl. I prepare our cereal, juice, and water for the coffee maker on a tray to take up to il nido.

I pour Gaines' first cup. "You look nice today. I like your tie and that sport jacket together."

He looks down at his tie, unaware of which one he had selected this morning. "I saw Sofia leaving Isabella's house this morning as Bridgie and I came back."

"Oh, well. It seems Isabella has a ghost who talks to her and tells her not to come inside of her house. Yesterday at caffé, Totó suggested that Sofia should go down and spend the night with her."

"You mean she really believes she has a ghost?"

"Yes. Yesterday she stood outside of her house, afraid to go in. I saw her two times standing out there in the cold. She had on her coat, scarf, and gloves, but she still looked frozen."

After riposo Bridgie and I are the last ones to arrive for caffé. Sofia lets us inside. "Briginella, *come stai?*" she says to the dog, who looks up to the large woman responding, "now," in her deep voice. Everyone laughs. "You all right, me darlin'?" She squeezes me so hard I swear I'll hear my ribs crack. It reminds me of Gaines comment that you've never really been hugged until it's been done by Sofia.

Totó is pouring the caffé and a little Strega in each cup. "Sit down here." He touches the back of the chair for me. Bridget makes her rounds, receiving pats and admiration from Domenica, Tiziana, Stefania, the Signorina, Gabriella and Lucia.

"Well? I can't wait any longer. What happened at Isabella's last night?"

"*Allora, prima di andare a letto, prepara un panino col tonno e un bicchiere di vino per il fantasma.*"

"Before you went to bed, she prepared a tuna sandwich and a glass of wine for the ghost?" I question.

"*E Isabella, mette un pezzo di pomodoro dentro il panino*" (And Isabella put a piece of tomato in the sandwich), Stefania adds, laughing.

220

Everyone enjoys the new situation. It's the best entertainment in weeks.

"*Hai sentito il fantasma, Sofia?*" (Did you hear the ghost?)

"*No, ma, ho detto a Isabella questa mattina, svegliati e prepara il caffè per il fantasma.*" (No, but I said to Isabella this morning, wake up and prepare the ghost caffè.) The room is uproarious again.

"Does she really think she hears a ghost?" asks Stefania.

"No," says Totó, scoffing. "It's an old trick a lot of them lonely widows use, like, to make their children feel sorry enough for them to let them move in with 'um. You wait, it won't be long, like, and Isabella will be living out at San Cataldo on the beach. They can't put her in the insane asylum because them nutty doctors let everyone out and closed the place up!"

At first there are smiles and giggles around the room at Totó's remark. We wait for someone to go onto another topic of conversation, until someone again succumbs to unreserved laughter, the room becoming uproarious with hearty laughter. When we finally gain our composure, I realize it has been a long time since I've laughed that hard. I have forgotten how good it feels just to laugh. It's refreshing to be with people who make their own fun.

I can't put Isabella out of my thoughts, and I wonder where reality ends for her and the delusive imagination begins. Her belief in a ghost forbidding her to enter her own home to the point of obeying it and wanting to feed it is so far-fetched. Never have I encountered such bizarre thinking and behavior. Or is Totó right, is she deceitfully manipulating her son into taking her in with him and his family?

37

There are many shabby, diminutive doorways on Sepolcri Messapici, as on every street in centro storico. Deceptive limitation of leeway and connecting exteriors give no hint of the sparkling, scrupulously kept spaciousness held inside. This description is especially fitting for the home of Valentino and Teresa De Marco, a fiftyish couple with a nineteen-year-old daughter, Francesca. Teresa De Marco is a petite woman and can be observed scurrying up and down the street darting in and out of the miniature orifices, tending to the needs of her husband and daughter, thereby giving everyone the appearance of having a mission of the utmost importance. She projects a no-nonsense demeanor coupled with a vinegary bearing. She only returns salutations soberly, never initiating them and never exchanges pleasantries with i vicini. Needless to say, she is not a consort of the little clique, but it can be said that she is one reason for their alliance. They are all in agreement they love to hate her together. Valentino, on the other hand, tips his hat, smiles, and makes greetings and pleasantries but only if it is unbeknownst to Teresa. Francesca, unfortunately, is the spitting image of her mother.

A little of Teresa's and Totó's trouble goes back to early last March, when Teresa hired Totó to sit during the night at the hospital with her ailing, aged father. In Totó's descriptive account, "I falls asleep, like, and the old bloke fell out of bed and they sacked me!" Well, the old bloke died shortly afterward. The fall didn't do him any favors, but it certainly wasn't the cause of his death. He was well on his way to a funeral mass when he was admitted to the hospital. Teresa unleashed such a scornful attack that Totó said he thought he was back with his first wife, Joan Collins.

The De Marco's are only seven doors from Totó's gate, which is no more than twenty-five meters. The covey never remains neutral in a neighborhood controversy. They feel it is their right to get involved in an *imbroglio* (conflict.) This incident had provided the tension and emotional release they all needed at that time because things had been quiet long enough. The covey fervently met every day after riposo exchanging information on Teresa's comings and goings.

The antithesis of Teresa De Marco is Giovanna Bruno, who lives with her husband, Guido, and twenty-year-old son, Roberto. Their apartment is above the Signorina. Roberto is fulfilling his military obligation of one year. He is stationed in Lecce and is able to spend some weekends at his parent's home, as well as in the scorching embraces of his neighbor, Francesca. This relationship has brought disapproval from the covey and they eye the mismatch with intense concentration. It is, in their opinion, a romance between good and evil.

On Thursday mornings I have my hair done at the neighborhood salon. It is owned by a gentleman who was taken to New York City when he was an infant. English became his first language. His mother was unhappy there, so his father brought his family back to Lecce when Carlo was an adolescent.

Carlo has a lovely shop on the ground floor of his large house, which is located behind Totó's residence. He is eighty now and has left all of his clients in the care of his daughter, Pina, who runs the shop. Carlo always comes down on Thursdays to chat with me. He loves to reminisce about living in the Big Apple. When "Once Upon a Time in America" (a film depicting the city in the 1920s) is on television, he lovingly says, "That's my New York!" knowing he'll never see it again.

The hair salon is not only a place of business, but a neighborhood social club as well. Tosca lives nearby, and after shopping at the market she stops for a chat. Sometimes she takes peas out of a sack and shells them, or she might snap green beans while visiting and sharing recipes.

Anna is a seamstress who uses the shop as a pickup and delivery place for her work. It is always a hive of conversation and activity. It doesn't seem important to Pina for everyone to have their hair done who drops by because she already has a good clientele.

I shop at Rudiae Market after my hair is done. The stalls are housed in a large building just outside the old city gate for which the Market is named. There is a flower shop where I buy five sheaves of apricot-colored gladioli every week for the tall blue vase in the dining room. Other shops include a bakery and three butchers, one specializing in *cavallo* (horse meat), which I never frequent. Fresh fish is available on Monday and Friday mornings. Also present is a delicatessen, a stall offering notions and household cleaners, and there are four fresh fruit and vegetable vendors. To round out the market is the egg man, who also sells fresh sprigs of laurel, rosemary, basil, oregano, and mint. A shopper can buy as little as one carrot, and the vendor always throws in a little bit of parsley for the sugo.

I have completed the shopping and am carrying the full plastic bags to the car when I notice a truck loaded with wood parked nearby. *"Signore, quanto costa questa legna?"* (How much is the wood?)

"Trecentomila." (About $280.)

"Ne vorrei un terzo." (I would like a third.)

"Sì, sì, signora. Dove abita?" (Yes, Mrs., Where do you live?)

"Non lontano. Via dei Sepolcri Messapici. *Vuole seguirmi."* (Not far. Follow me.)

The man follows me home and I successfully park in a space across the street. The huge truck eases around the corner and backs up to the gate, bringing Totó and the gargoyles (the Signorina and Gabriella) outside.

The driver steps out of the cab and converses with Totó in the dialect. "He says it's not worth it to him to sell you just a third of the wood, like. He wants to dump it all."

"First of all, Totó, before he followed me home, he told me that he would sell a third of it. That was just a lie, thinking I'd change my mind once he got here. It only took us three minutes from Rudiae. It's not like it is that far out of his way. He wasn't doing anything but loafing down there anyway. I may not speak Italian very well, but I'm not stupid. If he won't sell me what he said, then you just tell him to get lost!" Totó grins with pleasure. I don't wait around but wonder how Totó is translating my message.

Later in the afternoon I hear Sofia calling me from the cortile. "Adriana, *scendi giu.*" (Come down.)

"It's a little early for caffé, isn't it?"

"Come on." Sofia motions me down. Bridget and I reach the cortile. I see Totó in front of the gate, directing a large truck which is backing slowly toward him.

He turns to me. "This one will sell you a third of his load. He wants a hundred thousand for it."

"Va bene. Totó, where did you find him?"

"Oh, he was just driving by, like, and I ask him."

I look at him skeptically. "Oh sure, and you're not about to divulge your source, are you?" Once again it is demonstrated that a native knows how to get what one wants. Something we will never be able to accomplish by ourselves. This gives Totó a certain importance and he loves having us needing him.

The wood is dumped in front of the gate. Totó, Sofia, Stefania and I make haste to carry the sticks upstairs before riposo comes to an end. The pile of wood will be an inconvenience to motorists and pedestrians alike.

"Where do you want it?" Totó asks.

"Let's stack it in the corner of the enclosed patio off the kitchen." Bent over, and carefully picking up the pieces I can manage without doing serious damage to my manicure or my lower back problem. My arms are full of carefully selected pieces and as I rise slowly, I'm confronted by Teresa De Marco standing on the other side of the woodpile looking straight at me.

"Oh! Buon giorno, Signora."

"Buon giorno, quanto costa?" She asks, pointing to the wood with her sour expression.

"*Centomila lire.*" ($90.)

"*Ah! Molto cara!*" (Too expensive!)

Teresa's daughter, Francesca, comes out of their house and joins her mother. For the first time I see the girl's unfortunate predicament which can't be hidden underneath a full-length winter coat. "Buon giorno."

Francesca murmurs a "buon giorno," lowering her head and acting backward.

I meet Totó on the stairs. "Well, did you see her out there?"

"I sure did!"

"They can't get married until Roberto gets out of the army, like."

"How come?"

"It's an Italian law."

"When is his time up?"

"About the time the baby is due, in another month."

It takes an hour, but we get the wood carried upstairs. I walk out to the front where Totó is sweeping up and give him a remuneration for his helpfulness.

"Thanks, Totó. I really appreciate you all."

"Why do you want wood when you already pay a high price to heat that expensive place up there?" He points with his thumb, cigarette dangling from his lips.

"We like wood fires especially on winter weekends, plus the fact it's a shame not to use those lovely fireplaces."

"I don't understand you Americans. Pay for someone to cook for you. Pay for wood when you already have heat. It seems a bloody waste to me!"

"Don't worry about it, Totó."

"I wouldn't pay anyone."

"Yes, we all know, Totó. You wouldn't pay anyone to feed you! That has been established, but not everyone can cook as well as you!" He nods in proud agreement.

226

38

Bridget and I arrive in the front room and all covey membership is present and accounted for. It is apparent that the daily convivial vibrations have been replaced with a more serious mood. Totó is perched on the side of the day-bed enjoying his foul-smelling weed.

"*Lei ha comprato un abito bianco da cerimonia stamattina!*" (This morning she bought white for the ceremony!) Wails Gabriella, misfortune written all over her face.

"*Disastro! Disastro!*" Lucia clucks loudly.

The covey is in an emotional state because Francesca is wearing a white wedding dress for her marriage ceremony.

"*Francesca, lei é tremenda!*" (She has a lot of nerve!) Domenica exclaims.

"Oh?" Totó turns to me while obviously enjoying the controversy and chuckling at the women.

"*Bianco solo per le vergini! Solo!*" (White is for virgins only!) chimes in the Signorina.

"Ha, ha, ha!" he laughs. "If that's true, nobody would get married in white! Why, me first wife, Joan Collins, he, he, was five months pregnant, like, when we got hitched. I never would have married her otherwise."

"Dad, hush up!" Stefania is incensed at his crude remarks.

"Oh, everybody knows it, like," He grins.

"Only because you advertise it!"

Domenica is upset about a big church wedding with all the trimmings and declares it is more tasteful to wear navy blue and have the priest marry them quietly with only family present and not flaunt Francesca's condition in front of the Blessed Virgin Mary.

"Well, it seems to me if I remember right," Totó says, "The Blessed Mother was in the same condition as Francesca when she was married."

"*Bestemmia, bestemmia*" (Blaspheme), Sofia yells, giving Totó a chopping sign with the side of her hand.

"Always the devil's advocate, aren't you, Dad?"

"Oh, can't you two take a little joke, like?"

"*Certo, noi possiamo scherzare ma non sulla Madonna!*" (Certainly we can joke, but not on the Madonna.) Sofia rises slowly, crossing herself, and looking rather wild-eyed at Totó, who has just stepped over the line. Everyone in the room quiets down because we know what's coming next. Sofia commences to rev herself up a little more and goes into Sofiaese. Her large body moves in and around the seated guests, everyone anticipating the spectacle of pontificating, gesturing, and histrionics. Sofia's style is unique and there is no show like it anywhere!

Tiziana and Stefania cozy up together to make plans for shopping for the wedding. They decide on black winter dresses and wonder what Francesca will give each guest as a *bomboniere*. Although the covey has been on the outs with Teresa for many months, they are sure they'll receive invitations from the groom's family. Even though they are very critical of the choices Francesca has made, only death would keep them from attending the ceremony, not to mention the five hours of *mangiare, ballare e parlare* (to eat, to dance and to talk) in a nice restaurant. There is nothing like an Italian wedding to fill an entire day with joy!

A week later Bridget and I have been summoned for caffé, and when we enter the room, we receive friendly greetings from everyone of the covey except Totó, who has donned his glasses and a very serious expression. He is perched on the day-bed and is actually peering into a book. I am simply amazed and wonder if our resident clown has taken up literature something other, that is, than the soccer scores and other people's mail!

He says, not looking up, for he is lost in his own little project, "Now, Stefania. if you would be so good as to fetch me a piece of paper and a pencil, like."

"What for?" She asks rudely.

"Don't sit there like a tub of lard. Get it!"

She gives him a flip of her hand under her chin first, and does as he tells her to do. Totó motions her into the chair next to him. "Now," he begins, "tell me the very first thing you dreamed."

"I saw Francesca inside of the Duomo."

"Describe what you saw first, like." He moistens the end of his pencil. "Was it the altar, candles, statue of the Madonna or what?"

"*É molto importante,*" suggests Sofia, who turns to the covey and translates what Totó has asked Stefania in English. He is purposely using English for my benefit because I'm still in the dark, but nevertheless entertained by today's events.

"I told you," Stefania says impatiently. "I saw it all at the same time. She was inside the church. There were candles, altar and statues. It was the Duomo; I knew where I was!"

Totó starts searching the well-worn dream book. "Girl *numero*? *Chiesa* (church) number 75 . . ."

Sofia interrupts, "Toe *non usare ragazza. Donna é corretto!*" (Don't use girl. Women is correct.) Ah, si, si, si, si, si. Now we needs *bambina.*

"Baby?" I ask. "Born or unborn?"

"Ya see, it's like this, Signora. Stefania had a dream last night that Francesca had the baby inside the Duomo. When we gets up, she is tellin' us about her dream, and Giovanna comes to the gate and tells us Francesca had a baby girl early this morning. She had it at the hospital, not the church, but what's importante is the fact that Stefania dreamed it. It's good luck if you dream something and it happens. So, I'm going to play the numbers on the lottery today."

229

What a life! I smile, looking around the room at my neighbors laughing about Stefania's dream, and the fact that Totó takes it so seriously. He is filling out the lotto ticket with the aid of the Dream Book.

Domenica and the Signorina are still talking about Francesca's choice of wearing white for her wedding.

Sofia says, "Toe let's open the box of chocolates."

"You don't need any candy, Sofia. You look like a bloody pig now."

"Well you act like one!" she says laughing, and makes an oink, oink sound.

Totó returns from the kitchen with a large box of chocolate *Baci* (chocolate kisses). He passes it around to all of us including Sofia.

Tiziana is sitting on the floor next to Briginella and sneaks her a Biscotti, assuming I have not noticed.

"I saw that, Tiziana."

Lucia says, "*Io spero loro hanno una festa a San Cataldo. Vittorio ha un cuoco superiore.*" (I hope they have the wedding reception out at San Cataldo. Isabella's son, Vittorio, has an excellent chef.)

"*Una camera di Ballo é bellisima!*" (The ballroom is nice.), offers Gabriella.

"Totó, did you all hear that explosion in the night about twelve-thirty?" I ask.

"Ah, si, si, si." he says, with a serious expression.

"I wonder what happened?"

"Well, you see Signora, it is the end of the year and the owner of that service station down there across from the school had the front of his building blown off. It didn't kill him or put him out of business, like, but he'll remember to keep his payments up, if you know what I mean. It was just a warning. We always hear a few explosions in the night at this time of the year. The business has to be settled by the end of the year, like.

"*Io capisco*" (I understand), I mummer soberly, shaking my head and appreciating the fact that the Mafia is a part of everyday life here. Everyone pays for space. They give up a certain amount of freedom for a strange kind of protection.

Regardless of the Mafia, I can't help but compare my neighbors with people I know in the States. These people seem as happy as anyone I know at home and they have much less. Proving once again that material things don't bring happiness. Being content in your circumstances is the secret to a happy life. We are so different, and yet I'm comfortable with them and feel I belong in this unusual web of relationships.

39

Gaines comes in with Bridget and slams the door behind them. He takes two steps at a time up to il nido, where he finds me enjoying my morning coffee. "I found some Christmas tree branches!"

"Where?"

"Down at that empty lot below the prison. It's the lower branches of trees that have been discarded there. There's a huge pile of them."

"I'll get my coat; we'll need gloves to protect our hands."

We select as many of the long needle pine boughs as we can carry home and spend the rest of our Saturday morning decorating the mantels, the iron stair railing in the house, and the security gate outside. These activities are supervised by Totó and assisted by Sofia, who brings several strands of colored lights for Totó to place on the greenery around the gate.

"It is beautiful, Totó, but will it be left alone and not stolen?"

He shrugs. "I dunno, you better take a picture of it with them lights on as soon as it gets dark 'cause it may not be here in the morning." He giggles.

I go down to the flower shop At Rudiae and have four large red satin bows made to tie around the remaining boughs. I hang them on the white stucco wall beside the French doors on each level of the house. The fourth is centered on the front gate. It is the only house on Sepolcri Messapici decorated and many pass to see it.

A few days later I'm browsing at the Christmas tree lot at the market. What starts to be a curious whim is turning into a serious project. A gorgeous blue spruce is screaming, "take me."

My better judgement tells me to walk away, but I'm not strong enough to turn my back on the tree's cry and know this is an impetuous thing to do, but after all, the roots are balled with burlap wrapping, and it can be set in the ground after the holidays.

I walk a few meters over to the pottery vendor, and there is the perfect container, a very large terra cotta square shaped vessel, displaying a traditional egg and dart design around the rim. It gives this ordinary flower pot a little class. I decide it is the perfect holder for the blue spruce. The tree salesman agrees to plant the spruce in my container and deliver it that afternoon after closing.

The tree is lugged into the cortile and up the stairs followed by three sets of eyes mesmerized at the new acquisition. I open the door and am confronted by how large the tree really is. I almost shudder at my obvious loss of perspective while in that great big parking lot. The exhilaration I experienced at the market is somewhat dampened, but it's too late now.

The two deliverer's expressions convey annoyance at committing themselves to plant this monstrosity and deliver it, ignorant that the service included eighteen steep steps. Huffing and puffing they set it down in the doorway before continuing the extra footage to the living room. I politely wait for their recovery and offer, "*acqua*?" They shake their heads no giving each other the dreaded nod and simultaneously hoist it, following me into the living room. They place it in the corner across from the fireplace, and it fills the entire space, but the high ceiling accommodates it very well.

Gathering   strands of miniature white lights and the recently bought Baroque tree ornaments, enthusiasm is returning as I start the prickly task of arranging the lights on the branches.

There is a familiar knock on the door. "Oh," I groan, "*lasciami in pace!*" No privacy here. On my way to the door, I admonish myself repeating be nice, be nice, be nice. "Hi, Sofia, Stefania! Come on in." They give the cheek to cheek greeting, as if we haven't seen each other for six months, and enter the house. They almost run into the living room, whereupon Sofia steps back exclaiming, "*Madonna, l'albero é gigantico!*" (The tree is huge!)

I ignore the remark and we go to work arranging the lights.

"Let's have some Christmas music," I say, and put a tape of Handel's Messiah into the recorder. The shared activity becomes a delight and very soon we are joined by Totó, who really gets into the spirit of things. By the time the lights are all arranged to his satisfaction, the "self-appointed director of decorating" is telling us where to put each ball, cherub's head, angel, and piece of trim.

After it is finished, Totó plugs in the lights. Stefania goes out to the kitchen to make caffé, and Sofia answers the door to greet Domenica, Tiziana, the Signorina, Gabriella and Lucia. Bridget is happy and greeting everyone who enters. I take the fresh *Pasta di Mandorle* (almond paste, fish-shaped Leccese Christmas dessert), made by the cloistered Benedictine nuns, from the box and serve the covey thin slices with their caffé.

Gaines returns from work, greets everyone and steps back to admire the beautiful tree when he realizes it is alive with roots! "What, pray tell, are we going to do with it after the holidays?" Everyone laughs because there certainly isn't any ground to set it in here at number 24 Sepolcri Messapici. "We will give it to Luciana. She has plenty of ground," I respond.

I go into the kitchen to put the Sanremo tape of 1988 in the recorder. I bought it last spring after hearing the music on the radio. There isn't a song on the tape I don't like. The winner of Sanremo this year is Massimo Ranieri, singing *Perdere L'Amore* (To lose the love). *Per Noi* (For Us) by Fiordaliso is certainly a favorite and *Io Per Le Strade Di Quartiere* (The streets are my lodgings), F. Califano, a song that always reminds me of the inebriated artist that hangs out in the streets. I'll never forget meeting him one night when I took Bridget out for her last outing. That song depicts him so well it is as if it had been written for him. Everytime I hear that music, I'll remember this house and my first months here.

I join our guests and Totó is speaking. "Gaines, there was this bloke in England and he was a bloody son-of-a-bitch like, always giving me some grief. One day I got fed up with it and I walks up to him and sticks this knife I had in his bloody belly. He didn't bother me no more like. Gaines and I exchange looks, not knowing how to respond to what Totó has revealed.

Stefania is embarrassed and says, "Mom, can't you do something with him?"

"Toe loves to play, you know that," responds Sofia.

I watch Domenica go to the tree, remove an angle and place it a little lower on the other side. She decides that another ornament isn't where it should be and proceeds to rearrange it as well. Her antics entertains Gaines and he puts his fist up to his mouth trying to conceal his amusement.

Totó takes another bite of the dessert and says, "Oh, when I thinks of all the women I could have had and passed them up, like."

Stefania translates his inappropriate remark to the others.

Sofia has had enough of his half-baked remarks and shoots him a look that lets him know he is treading on thin ice.

The Signorina peels with laughter saying, "*Tu sei un sognatore!*" (You are a dreamer!)

"Lui *é un porco!*" (He is a pig!) responds Domenica.

Totó enjoys riling the women and prepares for a smoke.

The familiar song "Italia" (M. Reitano) comes on the tape and we sing along with it.

As time passes, the tree's shedding process continues and no amount of watering discourages the elimination of its needles. By the time the holidays are over on Epiphany, January 6, it is evident to everyone that the tree is dead.

On the last Sunday evening in January, we are going to Norma and Tom's for a potluck supper with the Americans to watch a previously recorded Super Bowl game. "Something has to be done with that tree, Gaines, and soon." We are on our way out of the cortile, carrying the picnic hamper.

Totó swings the gate open wide for us. "Enjoy yourselves and I'll see to *la princepessa.*"

"Thanks, Totó."

"Oh, Totó," Gaines says. "If you will get rid of the Christmas tree, you may have the container it is in."

"It's perfect for your rubber tree," I add, looking at the unsightly bucket housing his plant.

We return about eleven o'clock and find the roots of the tree lying on a newspaper close to Bridget's water dish. I catch sight of the planter in the corner of the cortile, holding Totó's rubber tree. "You sure got rid of the spruce in a hurry. How did you do it?"

He answers with cigarette still in his mouth and his eyes squinting through the smoke. "I burned it up, like."

"Where?"

"Why in your fireplace!"

"Wow, I bet that was a hot fire! Good thing the house and roof are stone." I carry the hamper into the kitchen. "Can you believe that, Gaines? Burning that huge tree up in our fireplace?"

"I can believe anything he would do!" Gaines groans. "God must love Italians a little more than he does the rest of us. He sure takes good care of them! Darn, the phone seems to be out of order. I need to call my dad and see how things are with him. I'll try later."

The phone is out of order for three days and the "SIP" service man responds to our complaint. I go to Luciana's, leaving Totó to let the repairman inside, and when I return Totó is sweeping up in the dining room. He pauses, takes his cigarette out of his mouth, motions over his shoulder toward the living room, and very casually says, "The repairman was here, like, and he said, you're going to have to pay an electrician to come and rewire for another phone in there next to the fireplace 'cause all them bloody wires in that there wall is all melted, like."

"Ohhhhhhh! I wonder who is responsible for that? I can't afford you, Totó! Do you remember how long it took us to get the bloody phone? Hum?" Just then the buzzer sounds. I look out the dining room French doors and see Margie at the front gate.

"Come on in, Margie."

"Oh, kid! I had to come into Lecce to pick up our mail at the post office and decided to run over here 'cause I've been trying to call you for the last two days. Is your phone out?"

"Yes, we had a meltdown Sunday evening."

"A what?"

"I'll explain later."

"Well, what I was calling about is, I thought all of us ought to go out and celebrate the fact that we have been in Italy for a year and one-third of the contract is over. Chet suggested we all meet up at Al Bano's Restaurant on Sunday after church.

"That sounds great."

"We thought we could tell something funny or unusual that has happened to us over the past year. Can you think of something to share with us?"

"I could probably come up with a thing or two!" Looking at Totó, I try to stifle my smile.

FINE

Pasta con *Aglio e Olio*
Pasta with garlic and oil
Serves 6

1/2 cup olive oil
8 average sized garlic cloves peeled and sliced
1/4 teaspoon red pepper flakes
Parmigiano-reggiano cheese, grated or romano cheese
1 pound of spaghetti

Heat oil in a skillet and add garlic.
Saute until it permeates the oil but don't let garlic brown.
Add red pepper flakes.

Cook spaghetti until al dente, drain and add to the oil,
toss, serve and add cheese at the table.

Always use pasta made with semolina or durum wheat.

Fagiolini con gli Spaghetti
Green Beans with Pasta
Serves 6

2 pounds of green beans
1 can Contadina's Pasta Ready
 Chunky Tomatoes with oil, garlic and spices
1 Knorr Vegetable Cube

1 tablespoon liquid smoke (optional)
Red pepper flakes (optional)
11/2 cups of Campbell's Healthy Choice chicken broth

Place the above ingredients in a large pot.
Bring to a boil, turn down and cook until done.

Cook a 16 ounce package of spaghetti until al dente,
drain and layer pasta and green beans.

Fusille di Fegatini
Pasta of Chicken Livers
Serves 6

1 package chicken livers
1/3 cup of olive oil
4 cloves garlic peeled and chopped
3 bay leaves
1/2 cup white wine
1 Knorr Veg. cube

1 pound of Fusille, spiral shaped pasta

Heat oil in skillet, add garlic and saute,
add veg. cube, chicken, bay leaves, wine and cook
on low until the livers are done.

Cook Fusille until al dente,
drain and add to other ingredients.

Orecchiette con Rape
("little ears" of pasta) with Broccoli
Serves 6

1/2 cup extra virgin olive oil
1 cup fresh bread crumbs
1 pound broccoli florets and little stems, cut and cleaned
6 cloves garlic peeled and chopped
1 dried red chili pepper, minced
6 flat anchovy fillets
1 Knorr veg. cube
1 box of Orecchiette

Heat 1/4 cup oil in skillet over moderate heat
and add bread crumbs. When golden brown, set aside.

Heat remaining oil and saute garlic,
add pepper, anchovy and veg. cube.

Cook pasta and broccoli together until pasta is al dente,
drain and add to oil mixture. Mix well and sprinkle with
bread crumbs. Buon Appetito!

Penne ai Boscoiola
Pasta of the Woods
Serves 6

2 Tablespoons olive oil
6 cloves garlic peeled and chopped
1/2 cup white wine
1/2 cup heavy cream
1 can Contadina Pasta Ready
  Chunky Tomatoes with olive oil, garlic and spices
3 ounces fresh porcini mushrooms diced or
  1/2 ounce dried, softened in hot water,
  broth or white wine for 30 min.
4 ounces shiitake mushrooms diced
1 package of penne pasta
  (Some people refer to this shape as mostaccioli).

Heat oil in skillet add garlic and saute.
Add mushrooms, wine, tomatoes, cream and mix well.

Cook Penne until al dente,
drain and toss with other ingredients until well coated.

Rice (Balls) Croquettes
Serves 6

2 T. butter
1 2/3 cups Arborio Rice. Don't use any other type of
rice.
3 cups chicken broth
6 T. grated parmigiano
Salt and pepper to taste
1 egg yolk, beaten
6 ounces fresh mozzarella cheese, cut into small pieces
6 ounces ham or prosciutto, cut into small pieces
11/2 cups fine dry bread crumbs
Oil for deep frying

Melt butter in pan, add rice and brown over high heat.

Meanwhile, bring stock to boil, add rice a little at a time
over med-low heat and at the end of 15 min. the rice
should be very dry. Add parmigiano, salt and pepper
and turn rice out onto a board to cool.

When rice is cold, mix in egg yolk.
Form into egg sized balls, push hole into center and
put in mozzarella and ham then close.

Roll balls in egg and coat with bread crumbs.
Heat oil in a deep fryer until just before smoking.
Fry croquettes until golden brown.
Drain on paper toweling.

Serve hot, warm or at room temperature.

Rustico
Filled Puffed Pastry (specialty of Lecce)

1 tablespoon butter
2 tablespoons flour
3 cups milk
2 egg whites, beaten
1 can of Contidina's Pasta Ready
Chunky Tomatoes, drained
2 cartons of fresh mozzarella, cut into 1/4 inch slices
1 package frozen puffed pastry

Prepare pastry according to directions on package.
When thawed and rolled out, cut into 3 1/2 inch circles.
Oven temperature and time for baking is on package.

Make a bechamel sauce of the flour, butter and milk.
Make paste of flour and butter. Slowly add milk
and whisk over med. heat until thickened.

Place cheese, a tablespoon of drained tomatoes
and a tablespoon of bechamel sauce on a circle of pastry.
Brush beaten egg whites around the edge of the circle
and top with another circle. The *Rustici* can be brushed
with egg whites before placing in preheated oven.

(Please note that the filled pastries may take a little
longer
time than the package suggests).

Remove from oven when golden in color.
These are nice for breakfast or lunch.

Parmigiana di Melanzane Baked eggplant /cheese

1/4 cup extra virgin olive oil
Freshly ground pepper
Salt
4 garlic cloves peeled and crushed
2 pounds tomatoes (I suggest cans of tomatoes
  imported from Italy). The taste is more authentic.
2 pounds eggplant
10 ounces fresh mozzarella drained and sliced
1/4 cup chopped basil leaves
Parmigiano-reggiano, grated for topping of the recipe
Oil for frying
Wash the eggplant, cut off tops and slice crosswise.
Sprinkle with salt and arrange the slices on a plate.
Top with a weight and prop the plate at an angle so most
of the eggplant juices will drain out. Drain for 2 hrs.
Dry eggplant and fry in 1/2 inch of smoking hot oil.
When golden, drain on paper toweling.
Heat the garlic in olive oil, add the tomatoes.
Salt and pepper, cook sauce for about 30 min.
Spread two tablespoons of sauce in baking dish.
Add a layer of eggplant and slices of mozzarella.
Scatter basil on top. Continue layering ingredients.
Finishing with grated Parmigano-Reggiano and basil.

Bake in a preheated 400 F. oven for 20 minutes.

Mimosa

Dessert for the Day of the *Donna* (March 8)

1 9 inch round sponge cake
2 cans of Thank You brand vanilla pudding
1 can crushed pineapple, drained
1 large container of Cool Whip
Shave the rim off the cake, crumble or dice and set aside.

Mix pudding and drained pineapple.
Top the cake forming a dome and cover with Cool Whip.
Sprinkle the cake crumbs on the top.

Refrigerate.

Pasta di Mandorle
Almond Dessert of the Benedictine Nuns
of Lecce

2 cups finely ground almonds
2 cups sugar
1/3 - 1/2 cup Amaretto
1 cup semi-sweet Ghiridelli chocolate

Put the chocolate in a double boiler and melt.
Grind almonds very fine.

Mix the almonds and sugar thoroughly
and add a splash of amaretto. Use your own
judgement on this because it is to be
moist but not wet.

Press half the mixture into half the mold.
   (Lamb shape for Easter, Fish shape for Christmas.)

Spread half the chocolate over almond mixture
and put the remaining recipe into the mold.

Place a lace paper doily on a serving plate or tray
and turn the recipe out of the mold.
Spread remaining chocolate on the top.

Keep dessert at room temperature,
but sealed tight so it won't dry out.
Do not refrigerate.

(Please note that this recipe is correct for my molds
and they were brought from Lecce. You will have to
adjust the amounts of the ingredients to your own
molds.)